THE Exquisite Egg

One Artist's Embellished Creations

Isabel B. Anthony

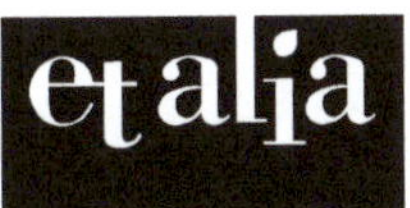

etaliapress.com

Little Rock, Arkansas

Dedicated to the many creatives out there and to
Erin and Isabel Wood, whose creativity is beyond the moon

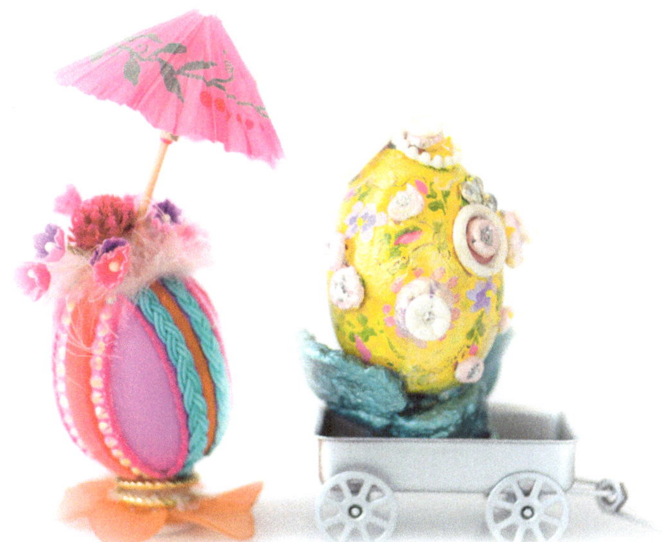

EGGSHELLS:

hen, goose, duck, turkey, emu, ostrich

TECHNIQUES:

decoupage, painting, embellishment

SUPPLIES:

paper, acrylic paints, metals, millinery supplies, vintage
jewels, metal chains, netting, miniature birds, whimsical
found objects, ribbons (velvet, moire, grosgrain, satin,
cotton, silk), wired ribbons

> "I think that, if required on pain of death to name instantly
> the most perfect thing in the universe, I should risk my fate on a bird's egg."
> —Thomas Wentworth Higginson, 1862

As an art form, eggs often symbolize life, renewal, and rebirth.

Whether a coffee-bean-sized hummingbird egg or an ostrich egg 18 inches in circumference, birds' eggs have simple, pleasing oval or round shapes.

For at least 65,000 years, eggs have served as canvases for ancient creatives. In South Africa in 2010, the earliest known examples of egg art were found; these beautiful ostrich eggs feature crosshatch designs and were used as personal water vessels, much like the modern canteen.

Probably the best known examples of egg art are the lavish creations of renowned jeweler Peter Carl Fabergé, commissioned by the Russian Imperial Romanoff family in the mid-1800s to the early 20th century. These enameled eggs are adorned with precious stones and metals and often have moving parts (a chicken flaps its wings, a clock ticks within an egg), and many unique floral and rococo eggs shine with jeweled appointments. The Imperial Eggs have brought tens of millions of dollars at auction from decorative arts collectors around the world.

In mythology and folklore, eggs have figured across time and geography. Hens' eggs represent the creation myths of many peoples.

Eggs were found in ancient Roman tombs. Jewish traditions use the white roasted egg as part of the Passover Seder Plate, representing birth, reproduction, life, and death, and ostrich eggs hang outside synagogues. The Passover egg dyed red became the symbol of Christ's blood in Christian Mesopotamia (today's eastern Syria, southeastern Turkey, and most of Iraq). This was the beginning of the Easter egg tradition. Red eggs are still prominent in the celebration of Easter in Greek Orthodox traditions. Oestara, the ancient Germanic goddess of spring, is the source of the word Easter. King Edward I of England contributed to the custom of decorating eggs for Easter. During his reign in the 13th century, 450 eggs were ordered to be colored and decorated with golden leaf, after which the eggs were presented as Easter gifts to the royal household.

In America, traditions such as the Pennsylvania Dutch and German tradition of Distelfink or scratch-carved eggs dating from the early 1800s continue today. The Pennsylvania Dutch settlers originated the idea of a rabbit hiding eggs in the garden. Let's not forget the White House Easter Egg Roll tradition that began in 1814 when Dolley Madison, wife of President James Madison, began the event for hundreds of children, a popular annual custom in Washington, D.C. Mexico, via Spanish explorers, perfected a festive tradition of small toy- or confetti-filled eggshells called cascorones, similar to miniature piñatas. This tradition is said to have begun in China centuries before the Spanish colonials.

Colored eggs have ancient roots in Persia (modern day Iran). Red was a popular Persian egg color and red eggs remain today in religious celebrations in Russia and Eastern European countries including Poland, the Ukraine, and Romania. Many countries continue egg traditions: Turkey, since the 17th century used ostrich eggs for religious symbolic décor; Hollowed, carved ostrich eggs with floral and animal motifs were used in Iran in the 1800s as water vessels; Egyptians incised ostrich eggs for Christian Copts; Polish artists use a colorful wax resistant dye regional craft method (called pysanky) of decorating hens' eggs—yellow represents the Resurrection, black connotes suffering, and red symbolizes the blood of Christ; Aboriginal peoples of Australia do Kalti paarti carving of emu eggs; Germans enclose biblical messages in eggs with ribbons attached; and Japan has its Kokeshi, washi, and Satsuma eggs—all stunning examples of the decorative arts that are given as wedding gifts as symbols of fertility.

These are but a few fascinating glimpses of eggs throughout history. Humans love our eggs.

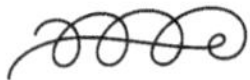

Do you remember as a child reading the Little Golden Books series, specifically Margaret Wise Brown's *The Golden Egg Book*? I read and reread this dreamy book as a youngster and still have an oversize, 1947, first-edition of Brown's book about the relationship of a rabbit to an exquisitely decorated, enormous Easter egg. My eyes also twinkled each Easter with the sight of my mother's golden egg, which she found at the St. Luke's Sunday school Easter egg roll in Hot Springs, Arkansas, in 1923; the first Easter following the publishing of this book, the golden egg will turn 99. It is pictured to the right.

My journey with embellished eggs began in the early 1960s, inspired by a *Ladies' Home Journal* article about Fabergé eggs, and continues 60 years later. Colorful remnants of French ribbons, millinery flowers, German appliques, sequins and beads of all kinds and colors, and even small-to-large faux-birds and feathers adorn the hundreds of eggs that I have enjoyed decorating through the decades. Many of my eggs have been inspired by and given to friends. Many others remain in my small art studio as reminders and warm memories of, for instance, my mother's hat collection, bridal bouquet ribbons, vintage jewelry, or other sentimental decorative relics.

Returning to egg art during the lonely, isolated early months of the Covid-19 pandemic seemed poignant and spiritually elevating. Honing in on eggshells with minutely detailed trimmings felt almost primal. Aesthetic choices like color, line, form, texture, and the ultimate joy of seeing a unique creation completely finished gave me hope. Hours of solitude forced me to examine myself and ask just what was important. Making something lasting, something future generations could treasure and appreciate, became my daily goal. I realized during those months of lockdown how few choices one could make in daily life, something that I had never experienced before. The choice to create *something* artistic every day seemed vital, so I dove into egg art like an explorer on a voyage to a foreign-yet-familiar continent.

French artists sometimes refer to inspiration as a coup de foudre, a stroke of lightning. Perhaps this playful book will inspire you to look more closely at eggs as a smooth canvas of inspiration and creativity? Maybe turning the pages of this book will become a family tradition at Easter time? Or perhaps my collection will become a source of artistic stimulation? My wish is that it will be your own coup de foudre.

Whatever these pages evoke in you, I hope you enjoy them as I enjoyed creating each embellished egg within.

—Isabel B. Anthony

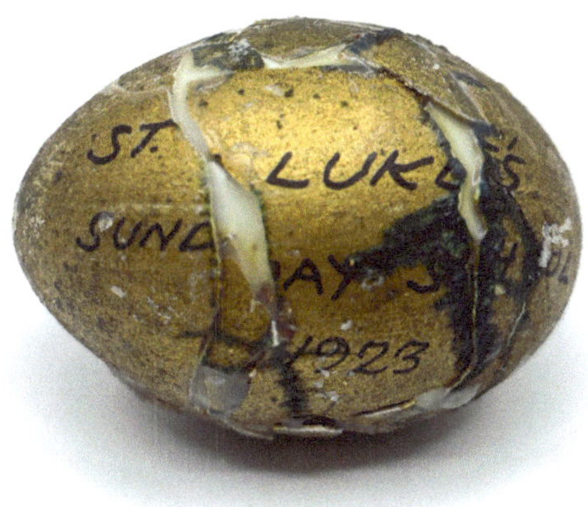

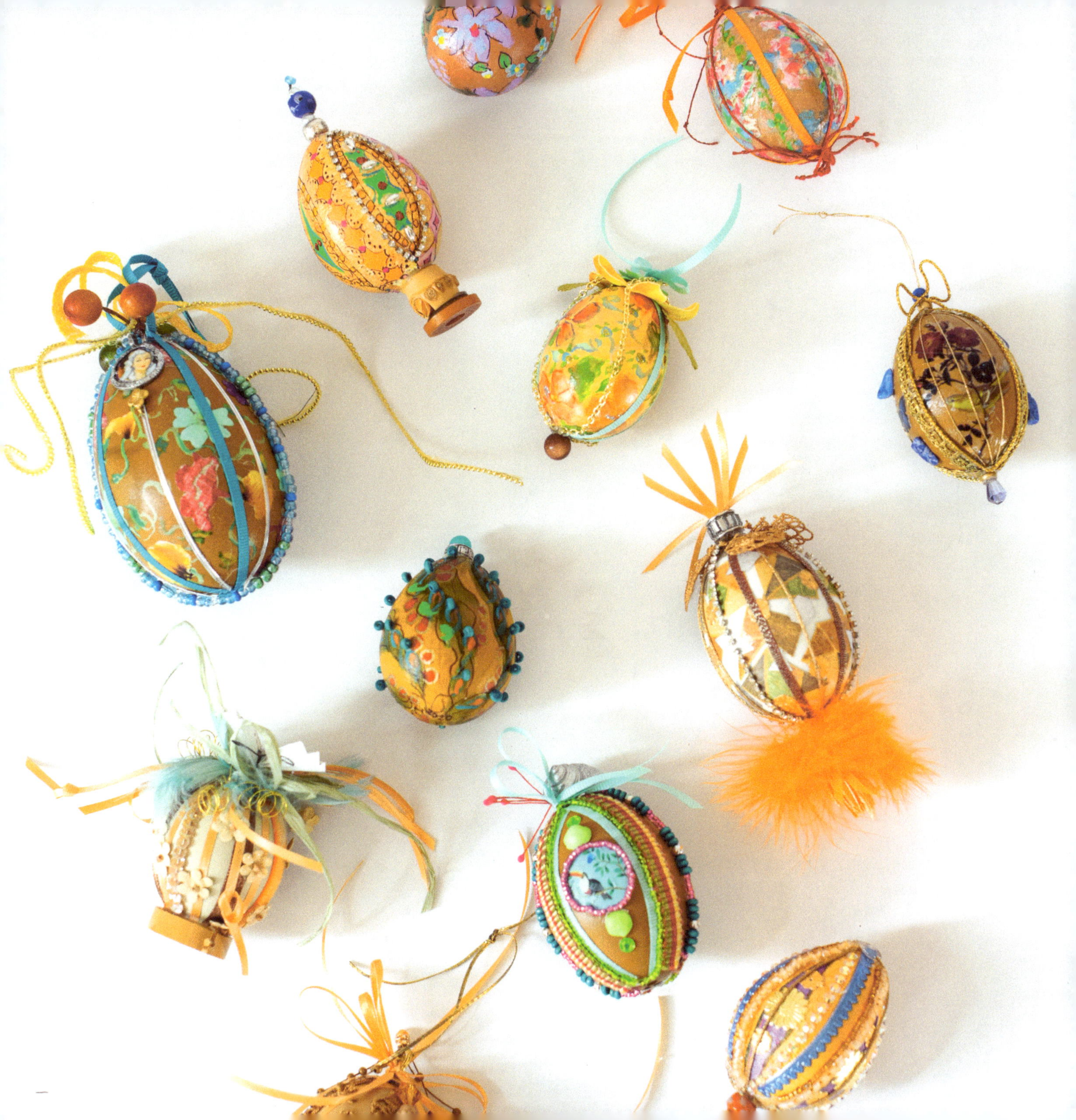

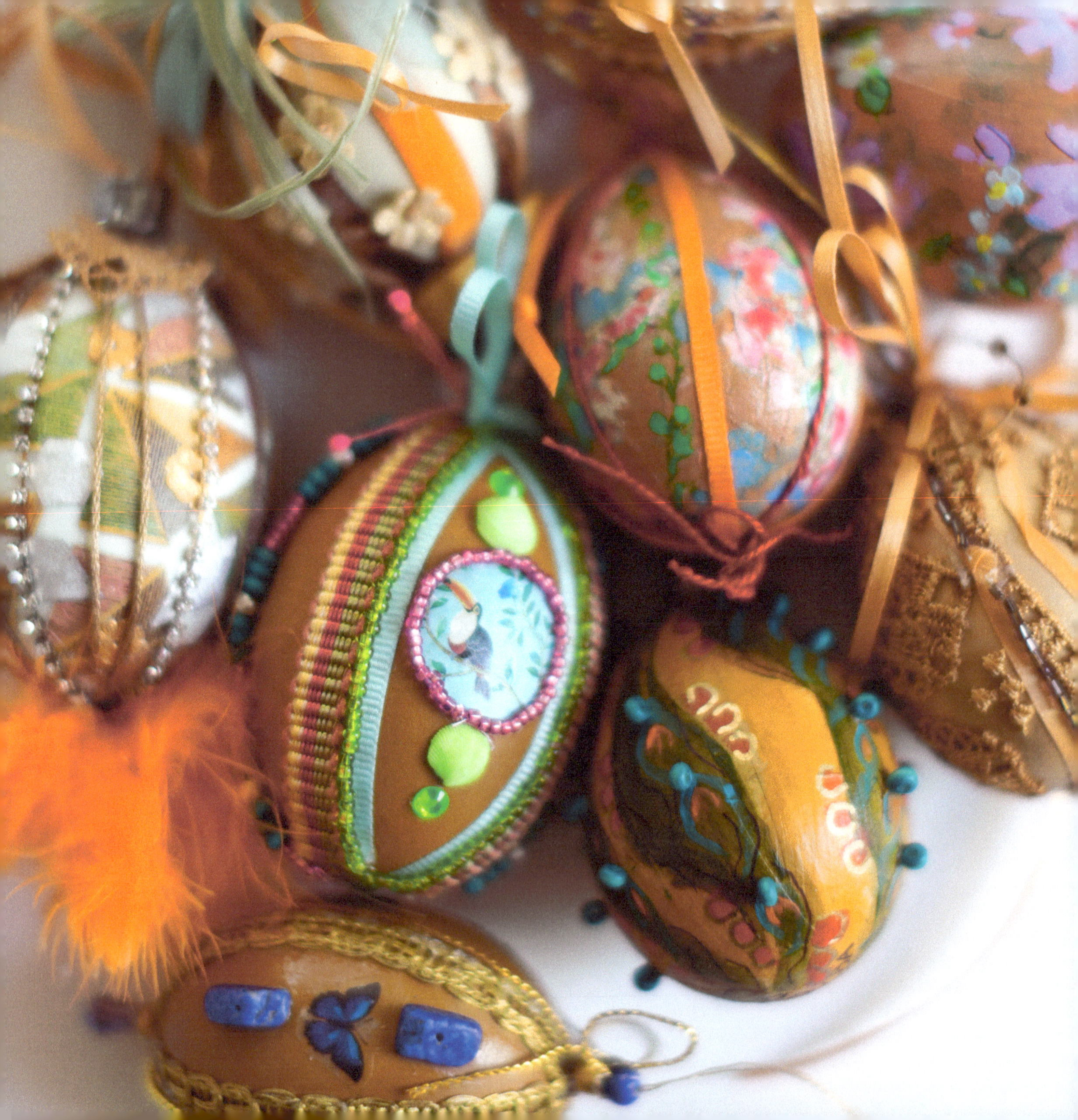

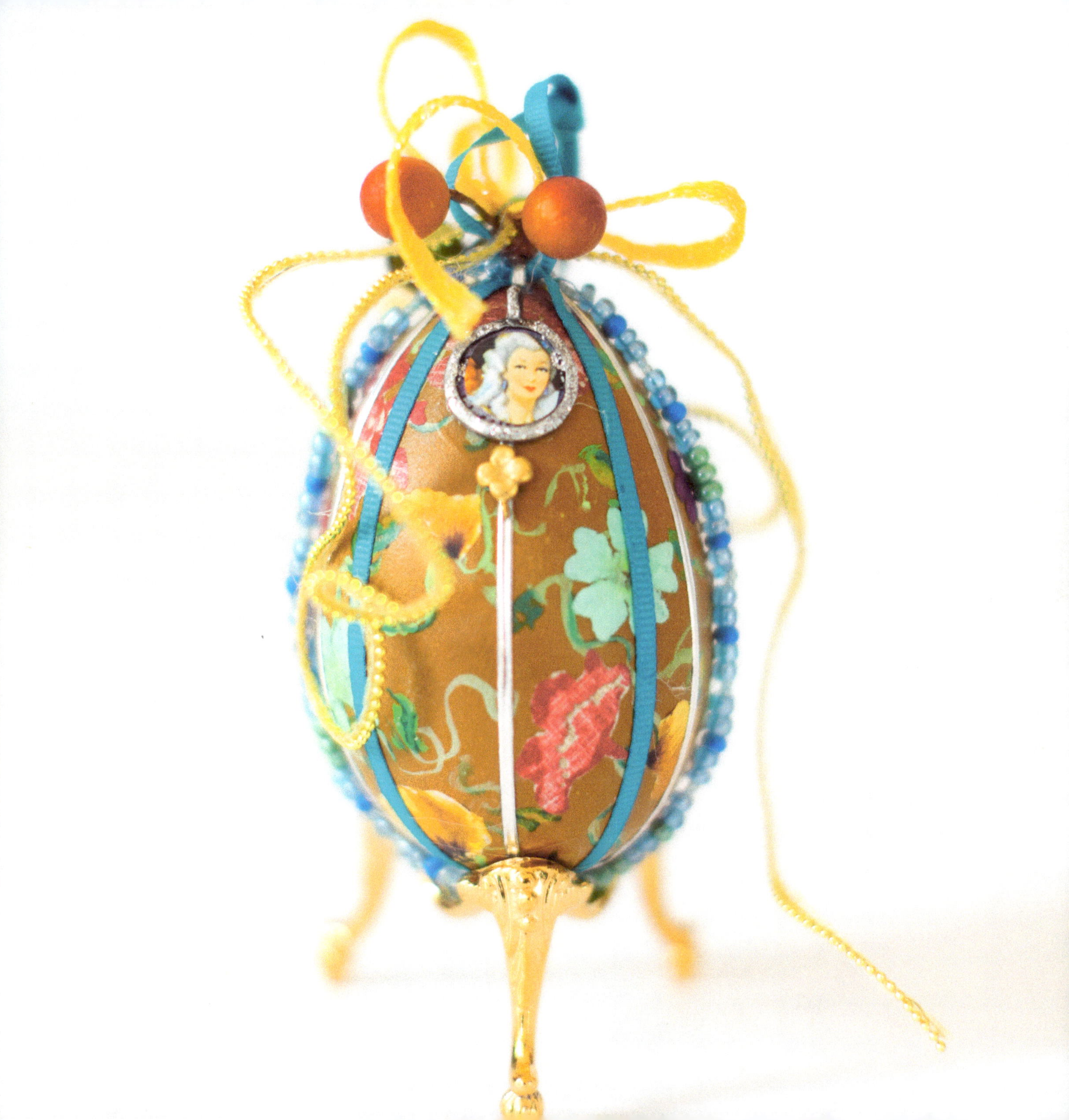

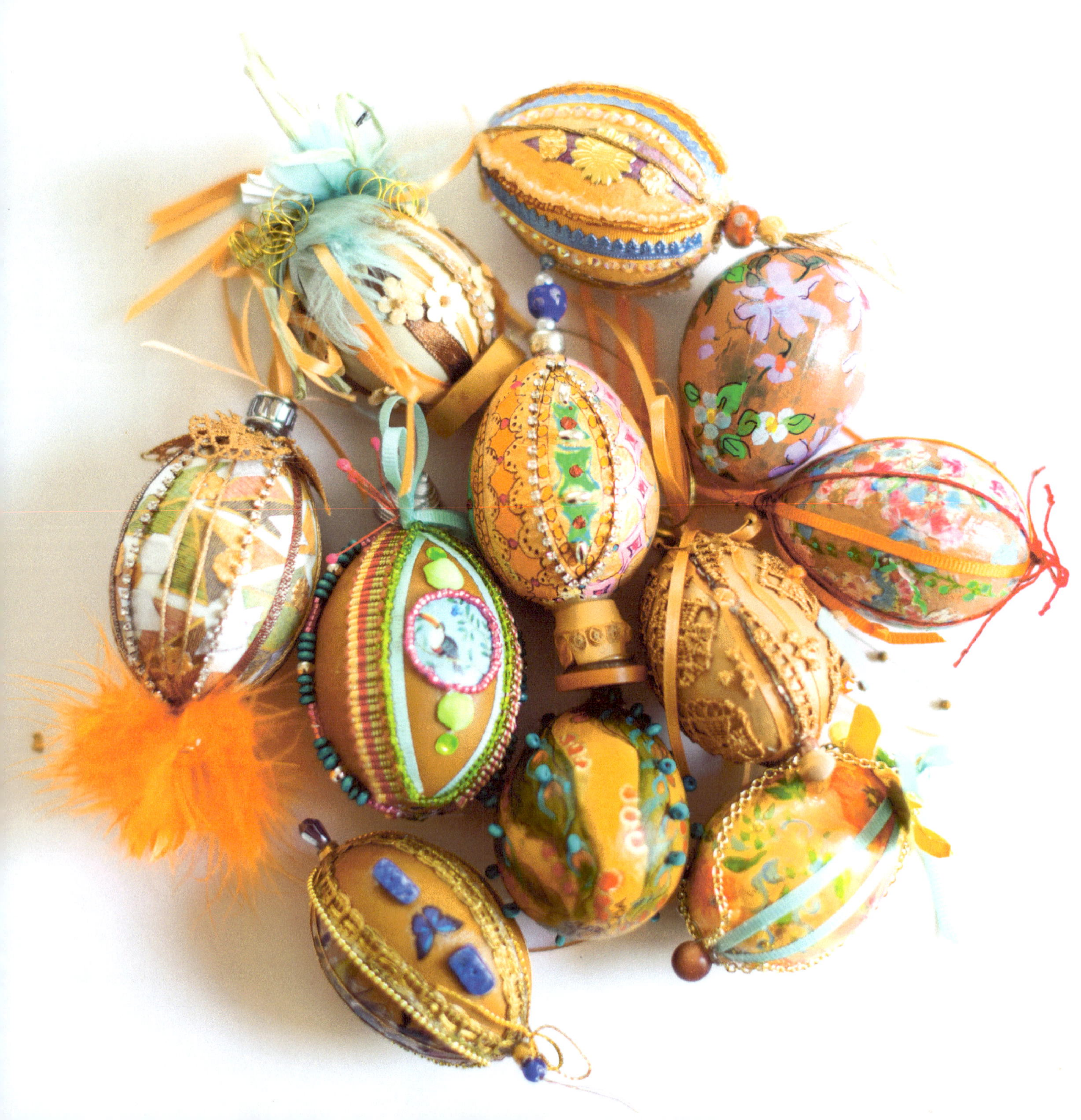

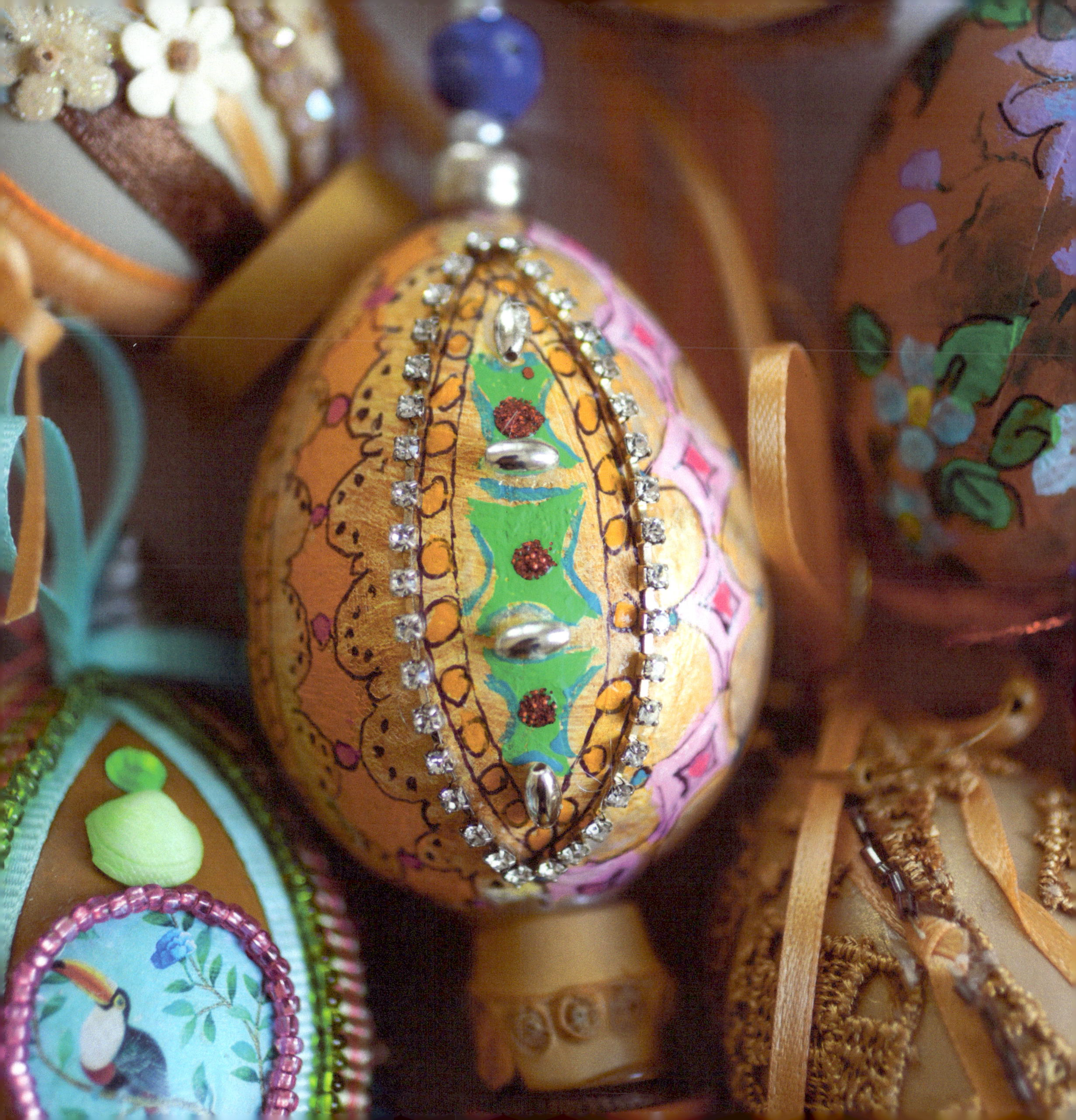

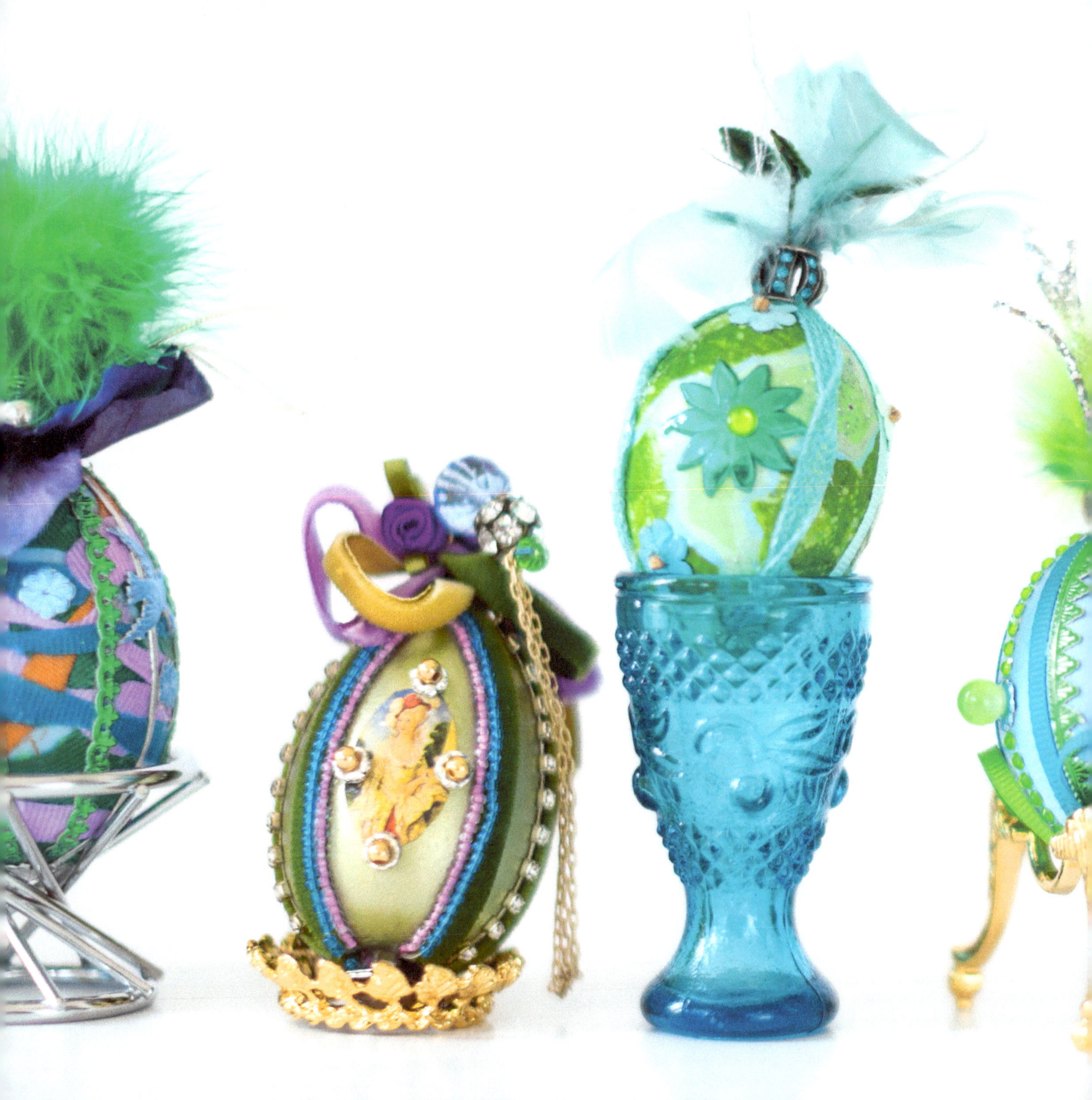

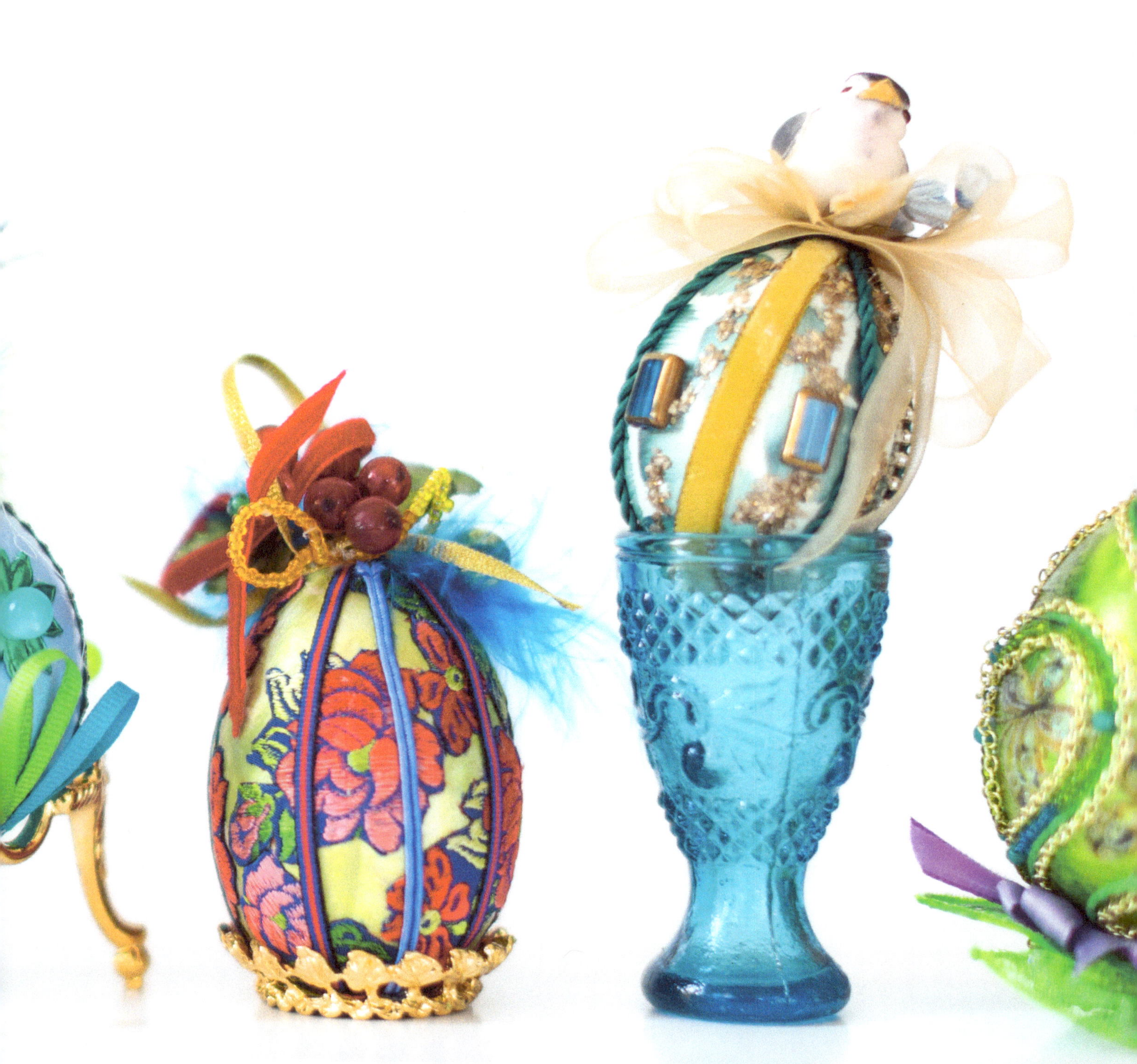

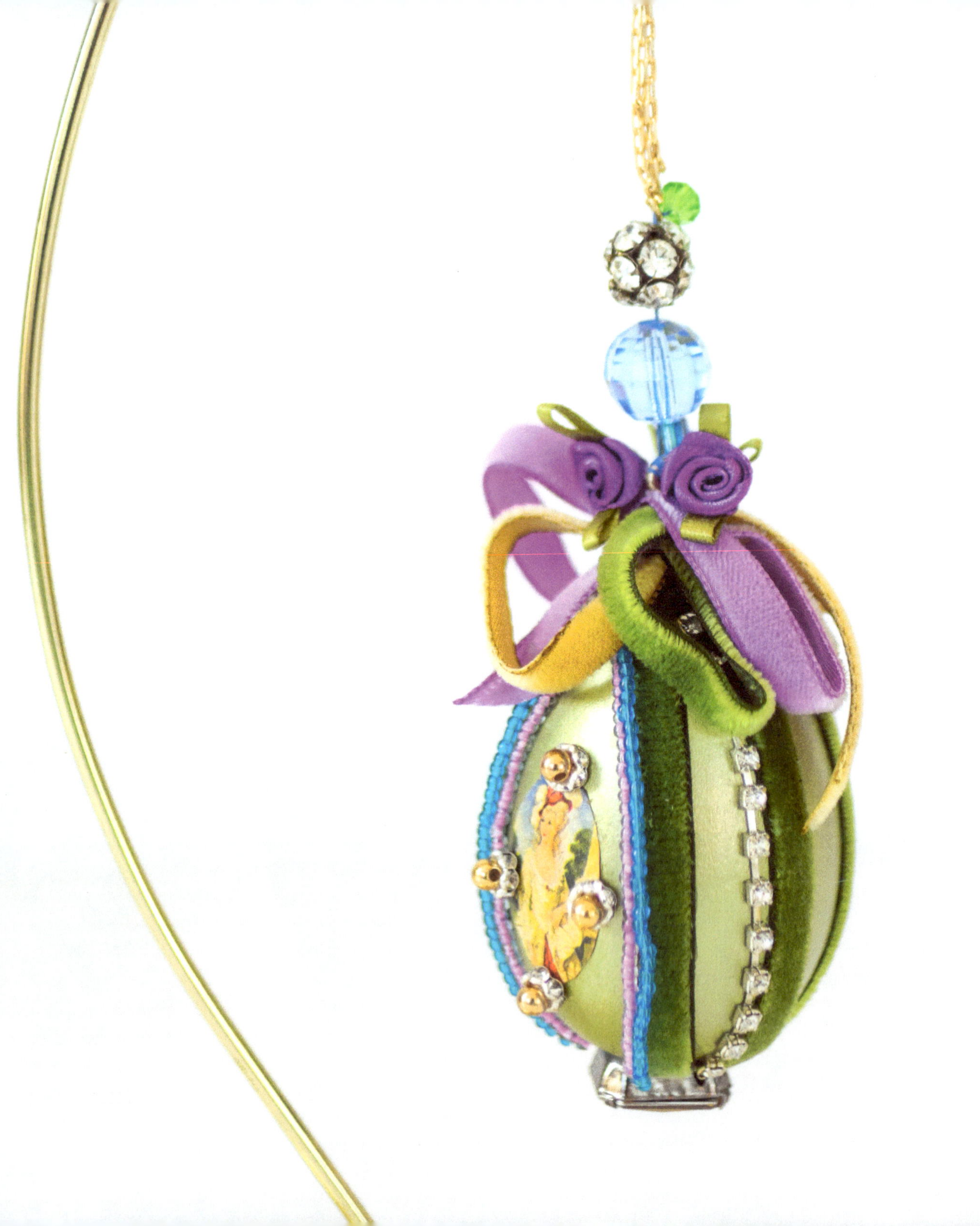

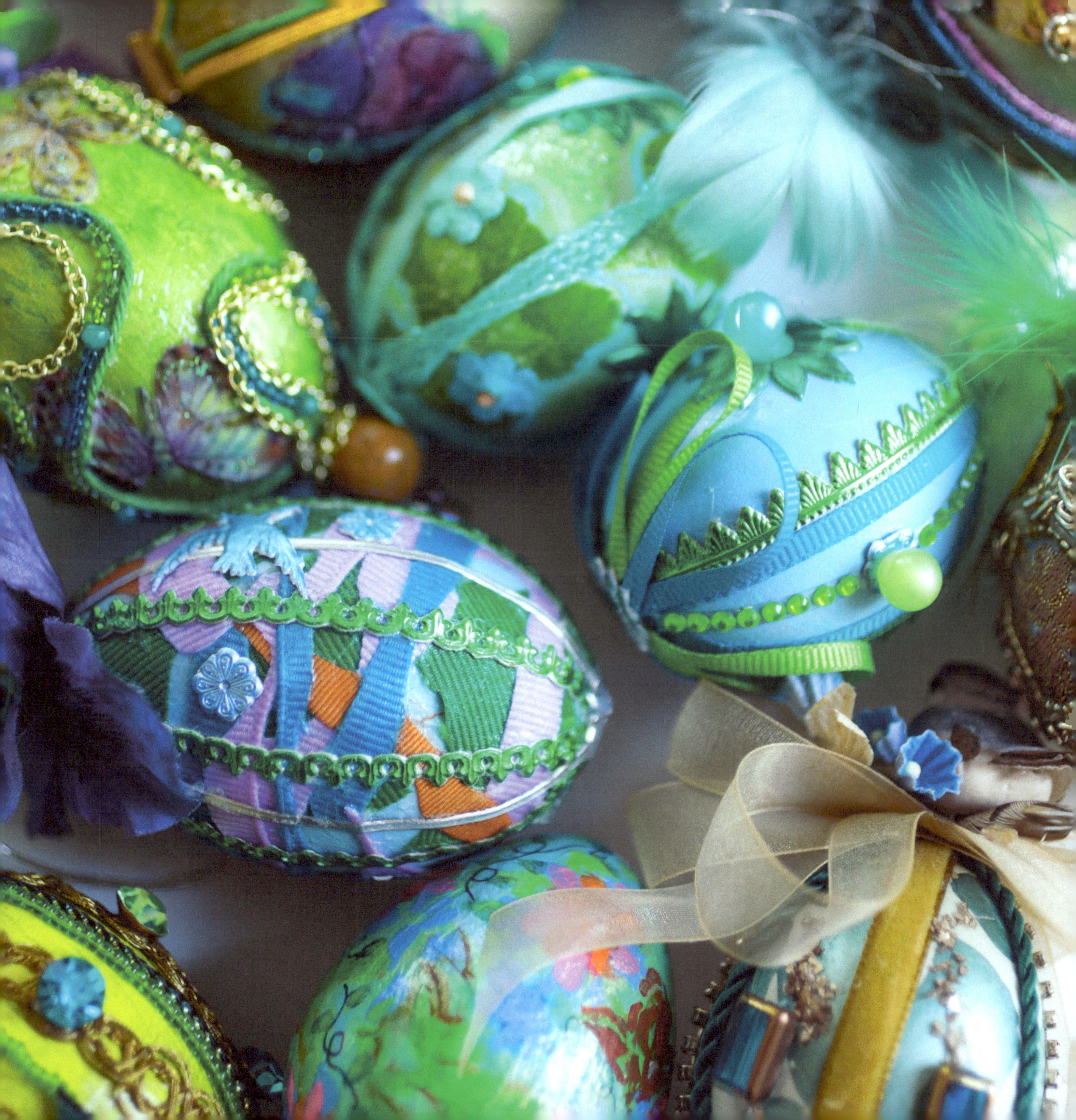

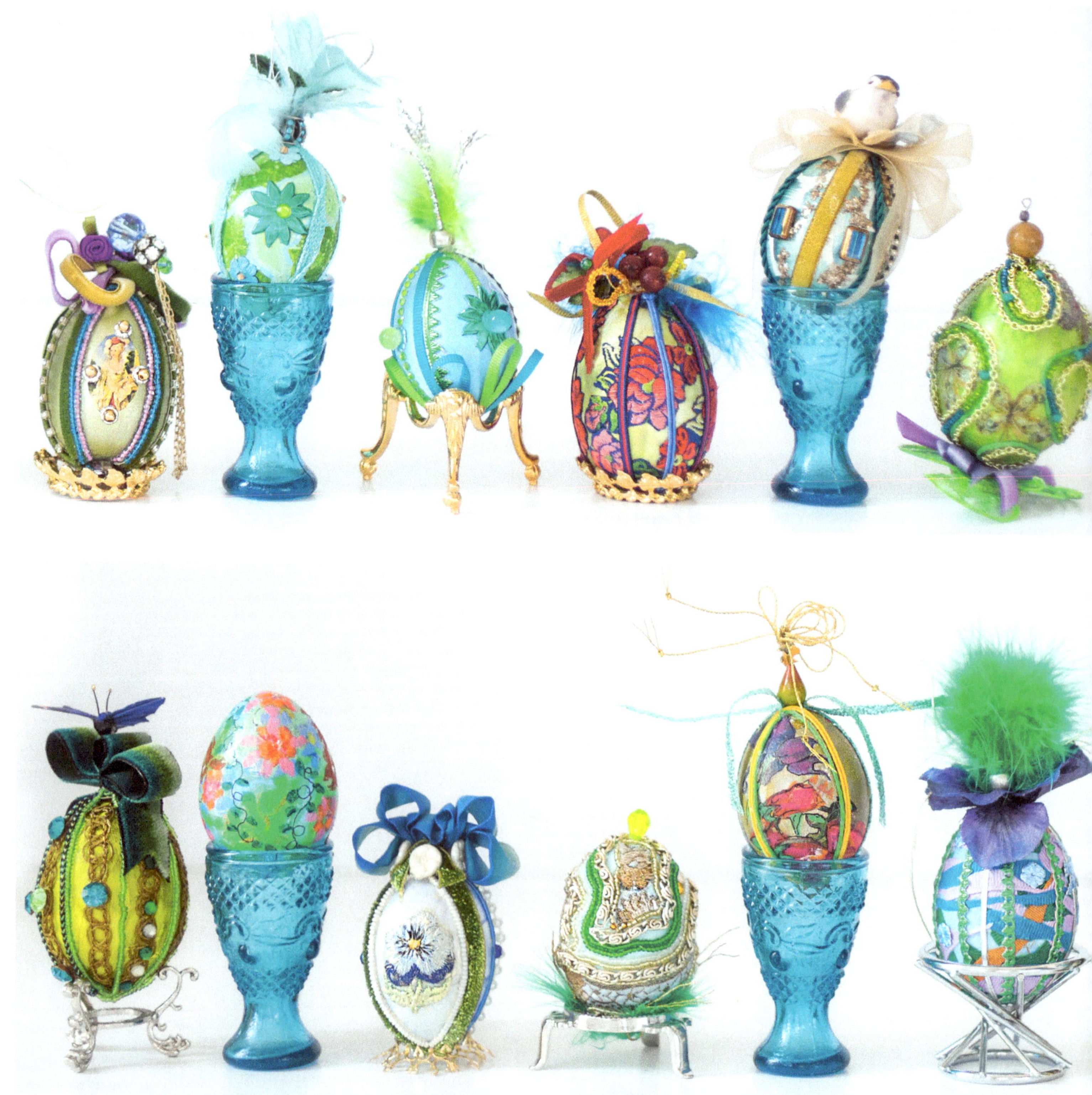

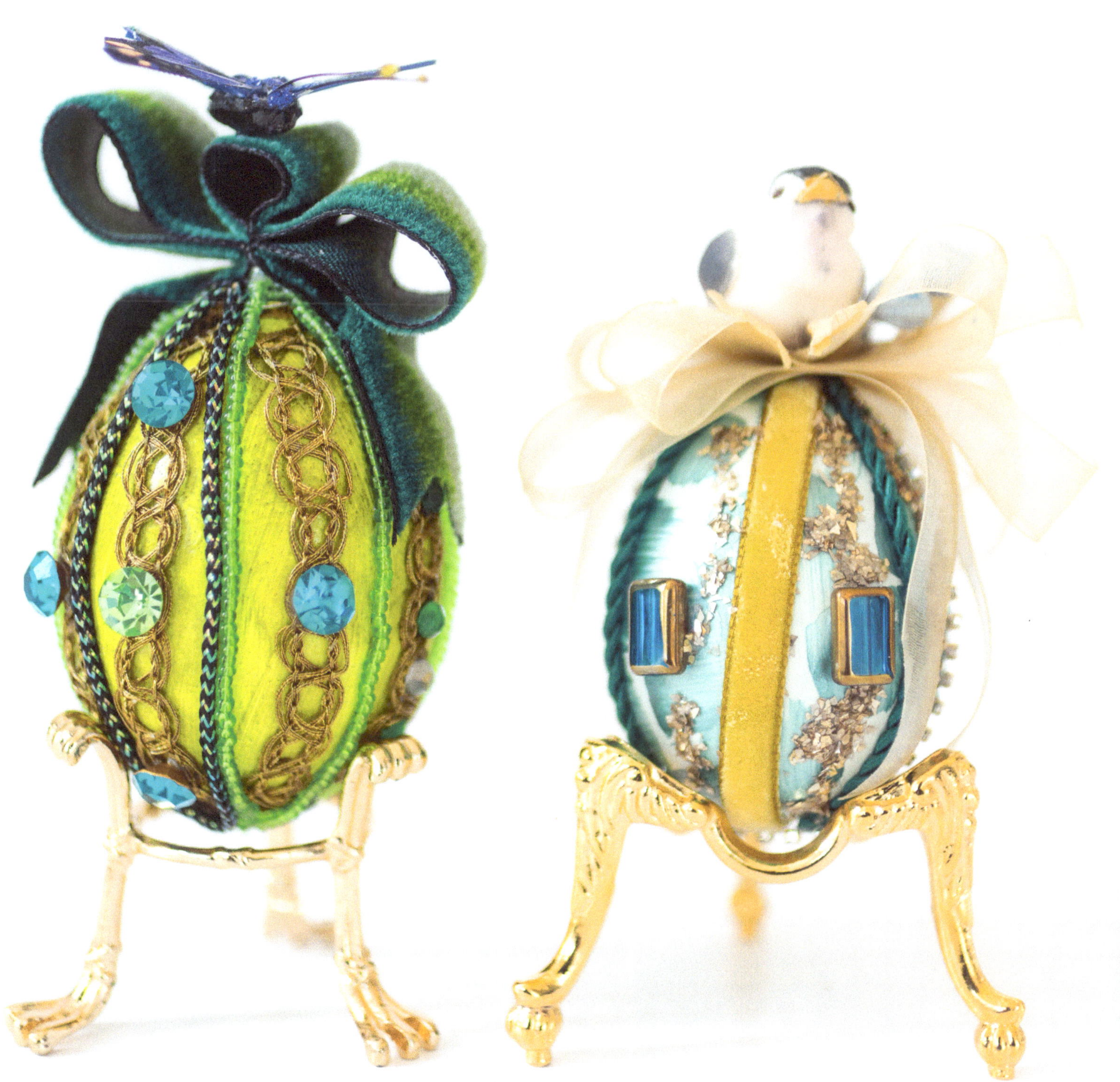

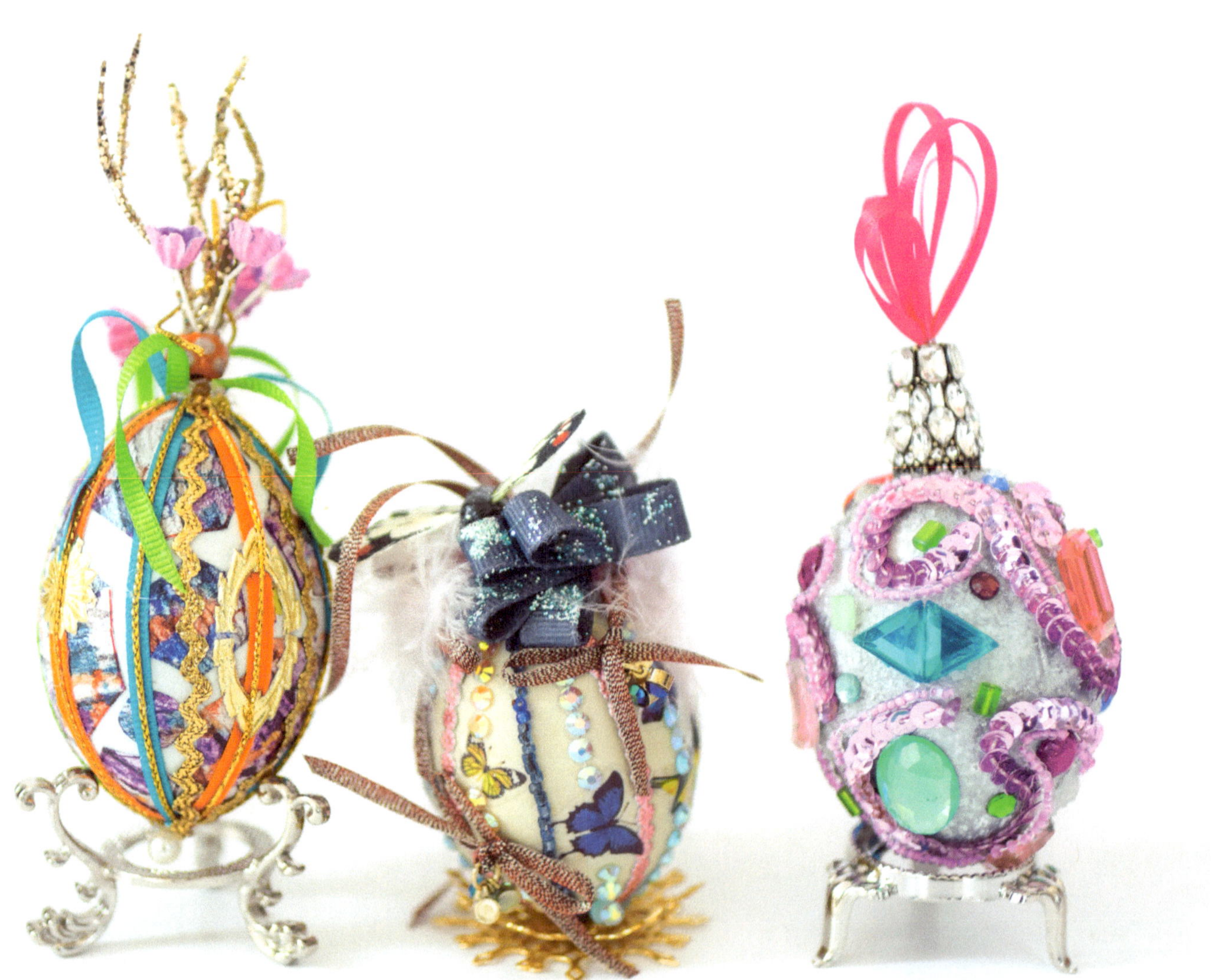

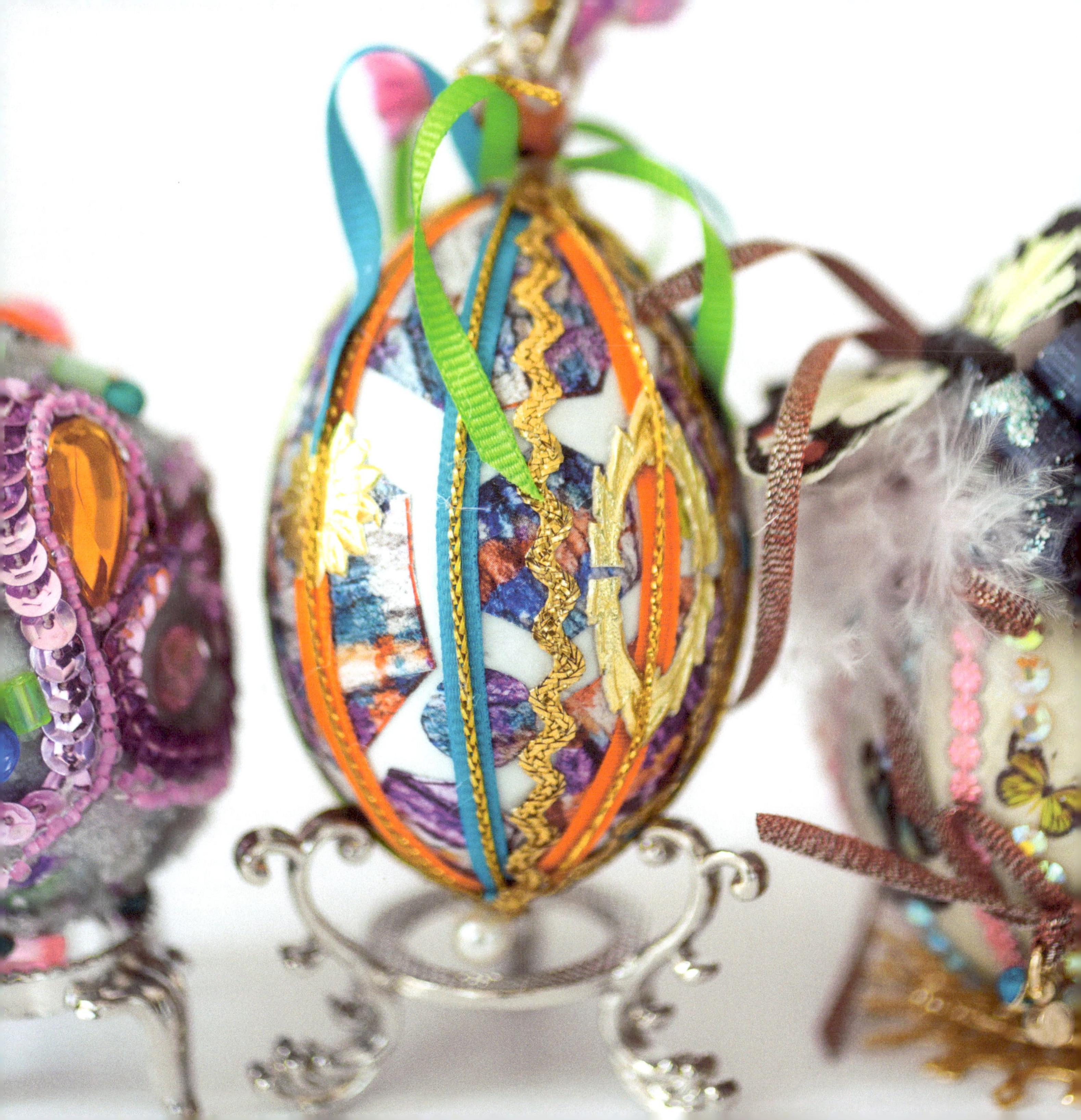

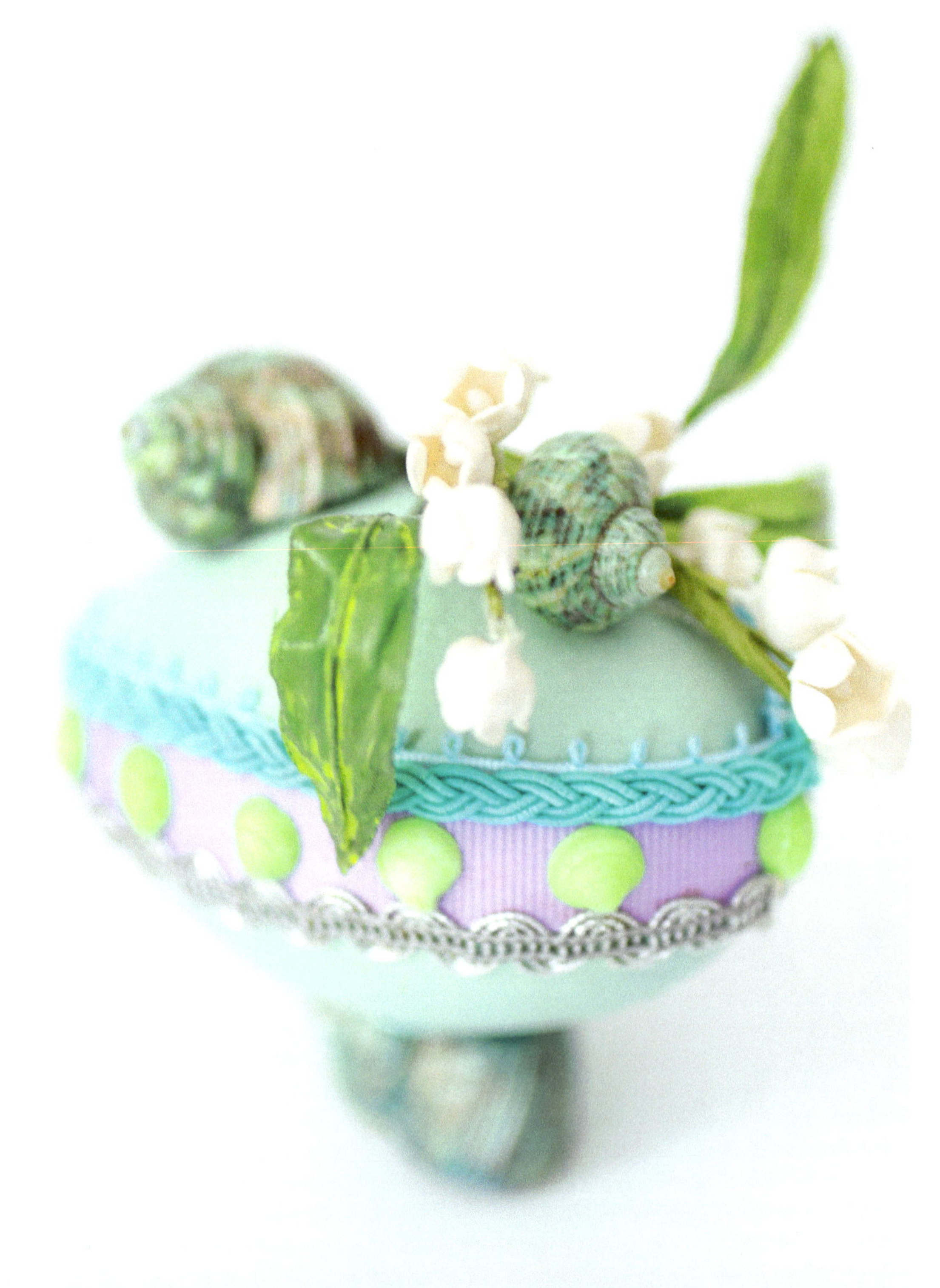

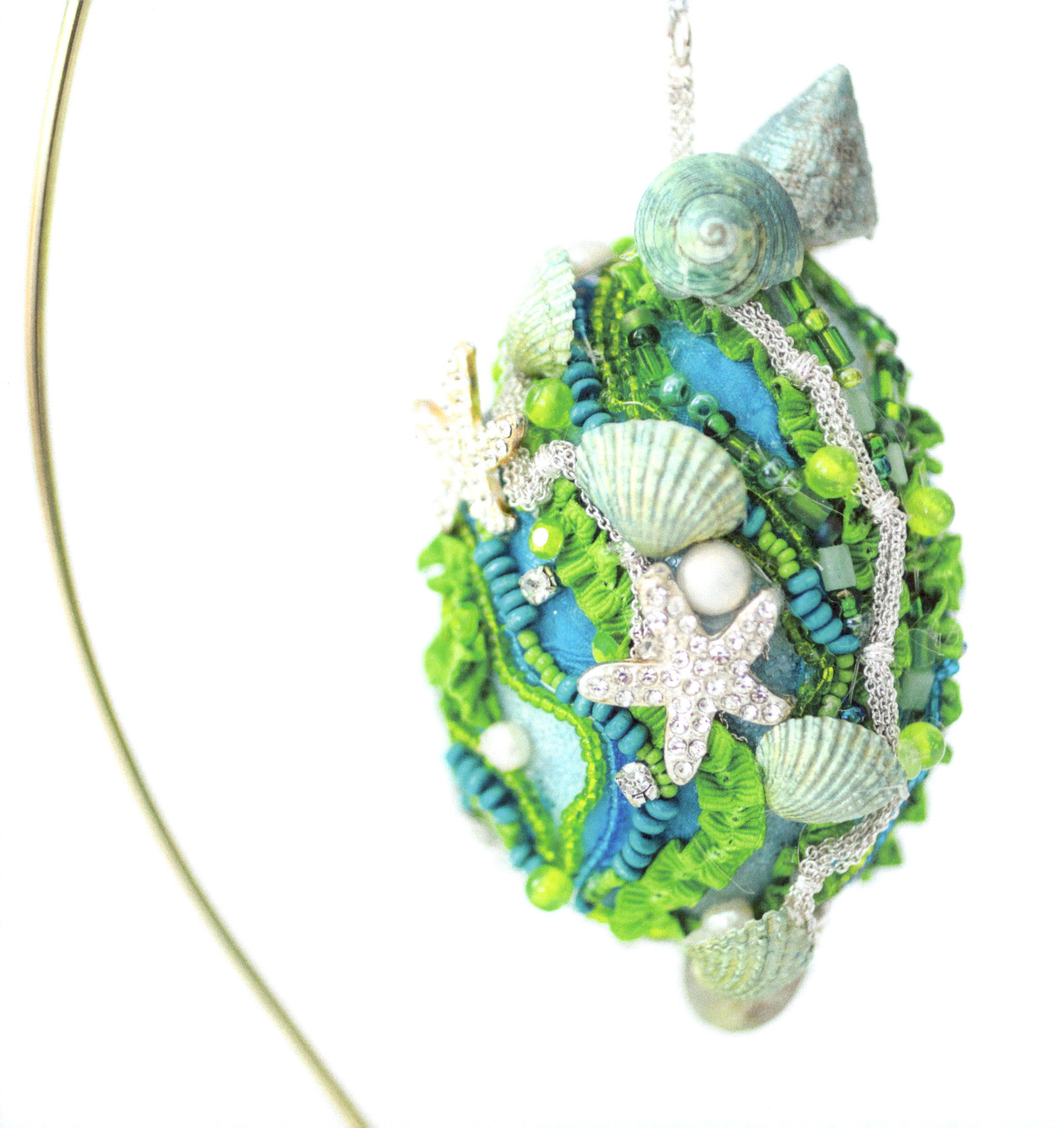

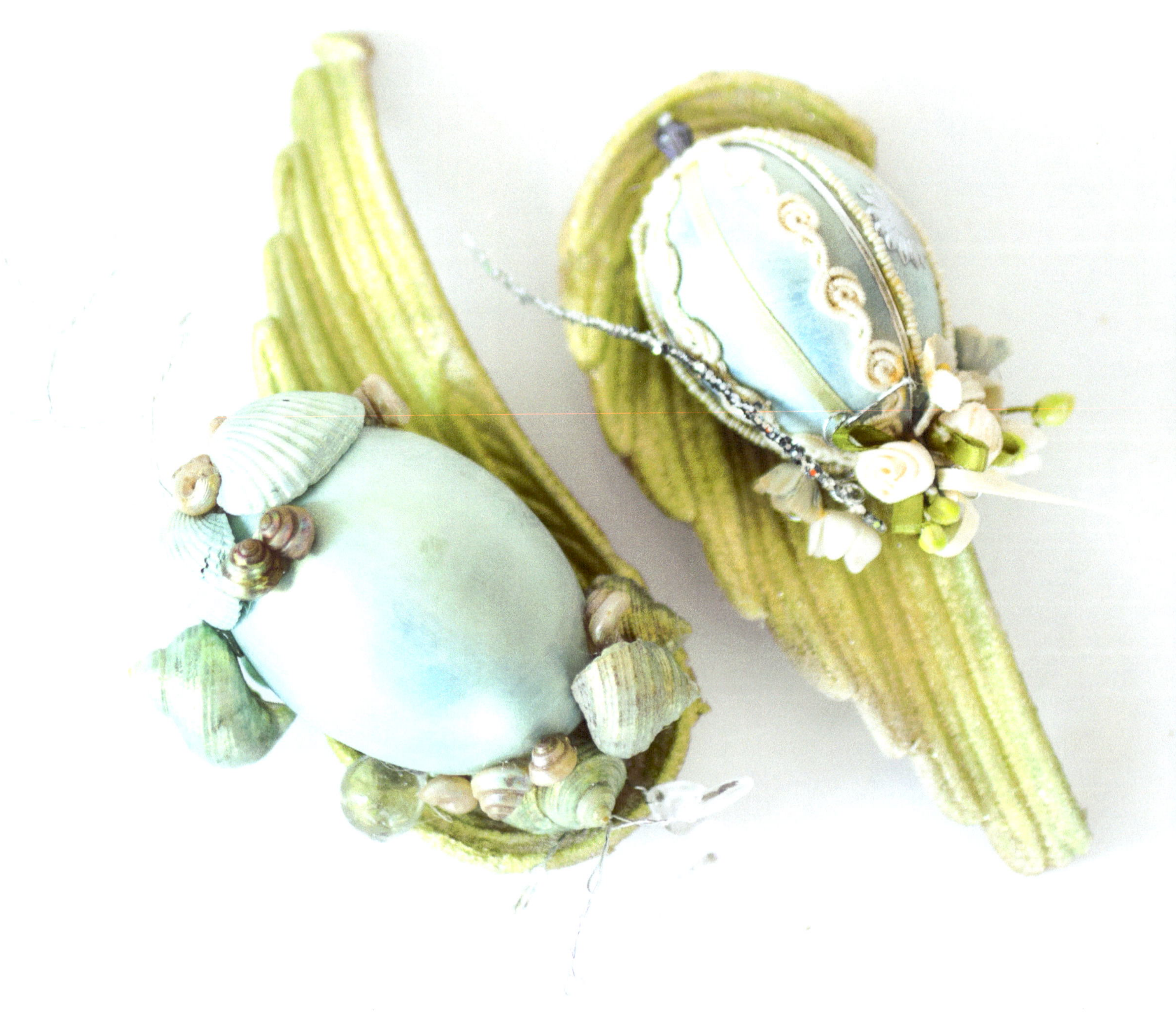

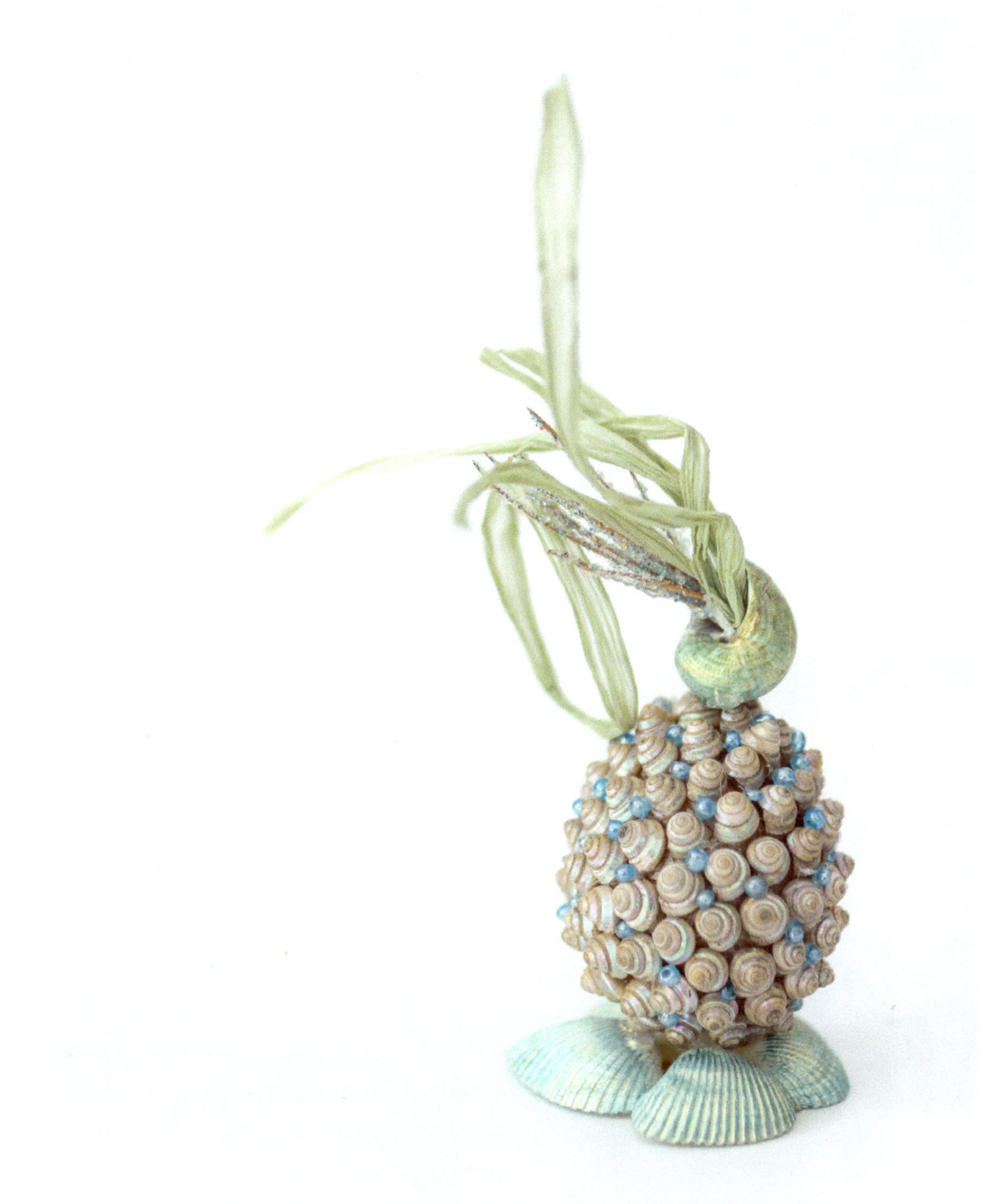

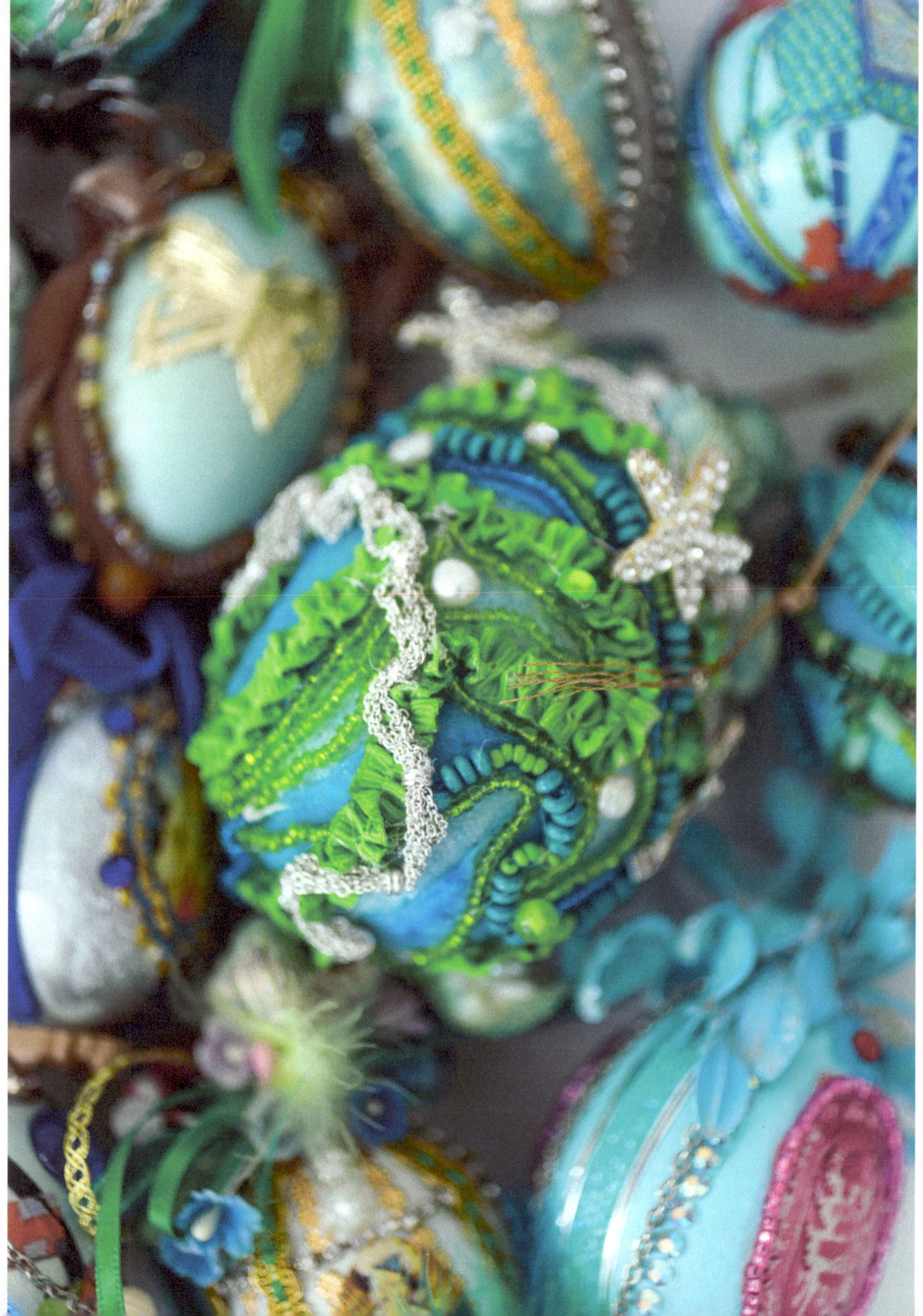

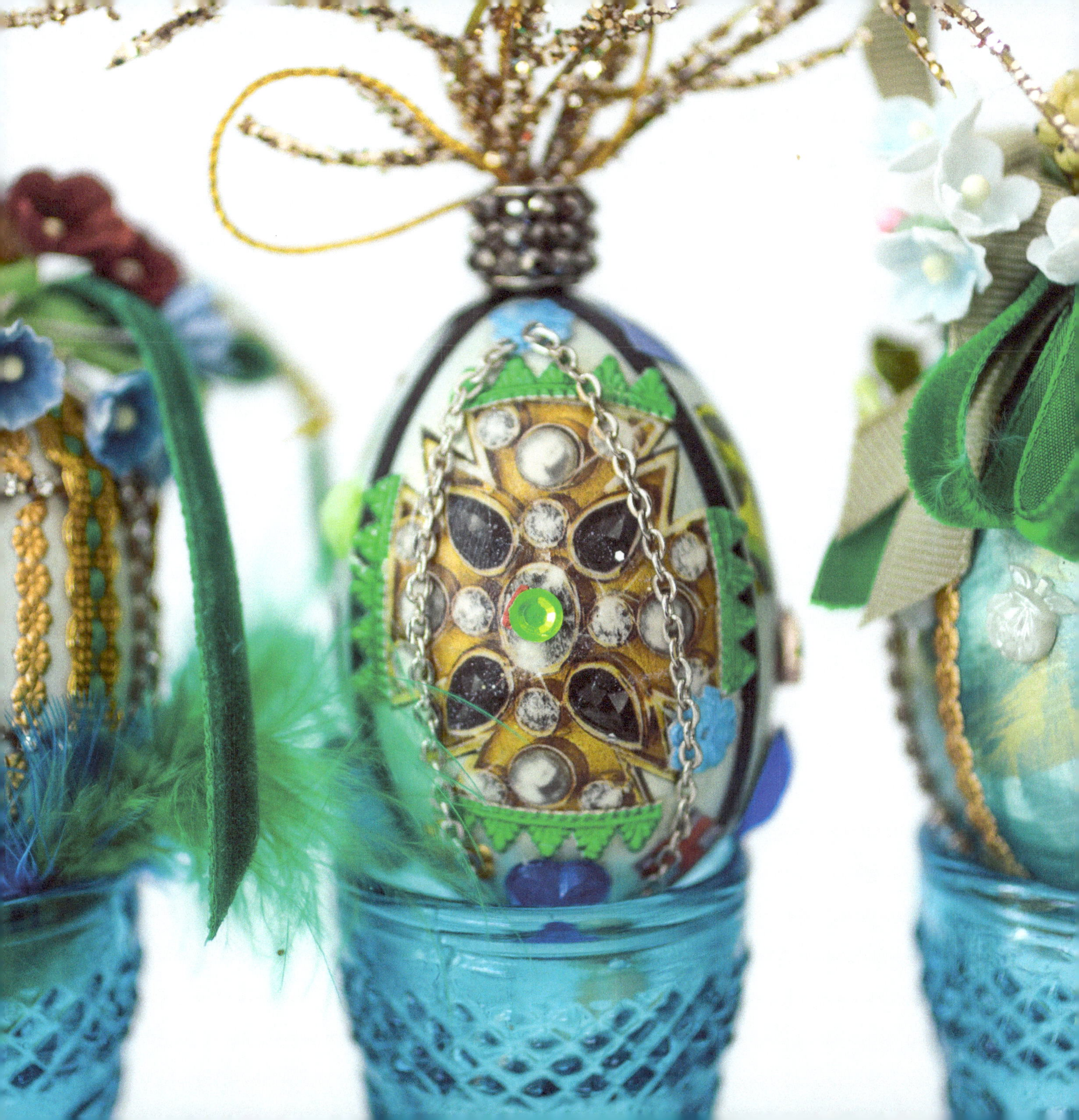

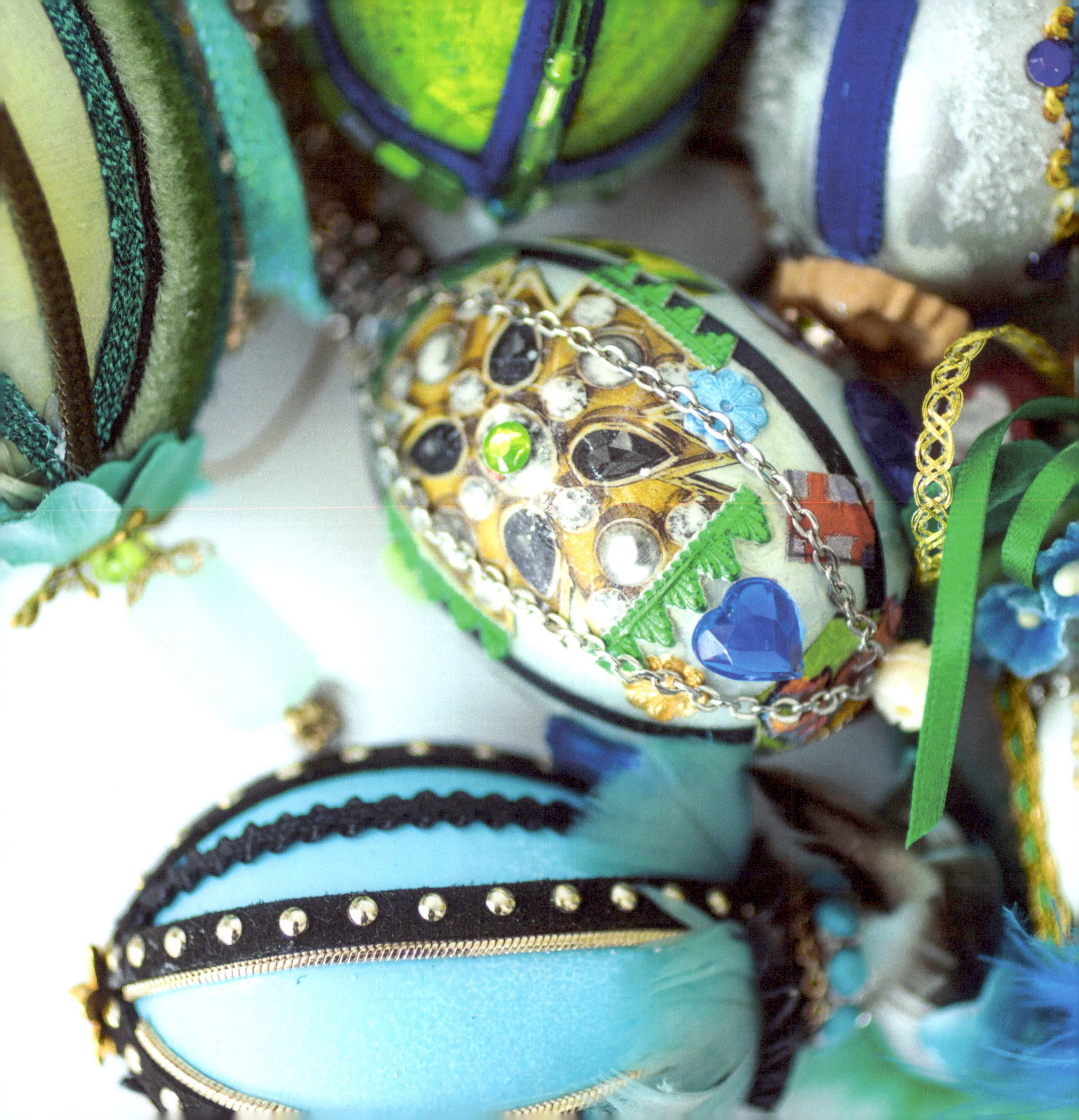

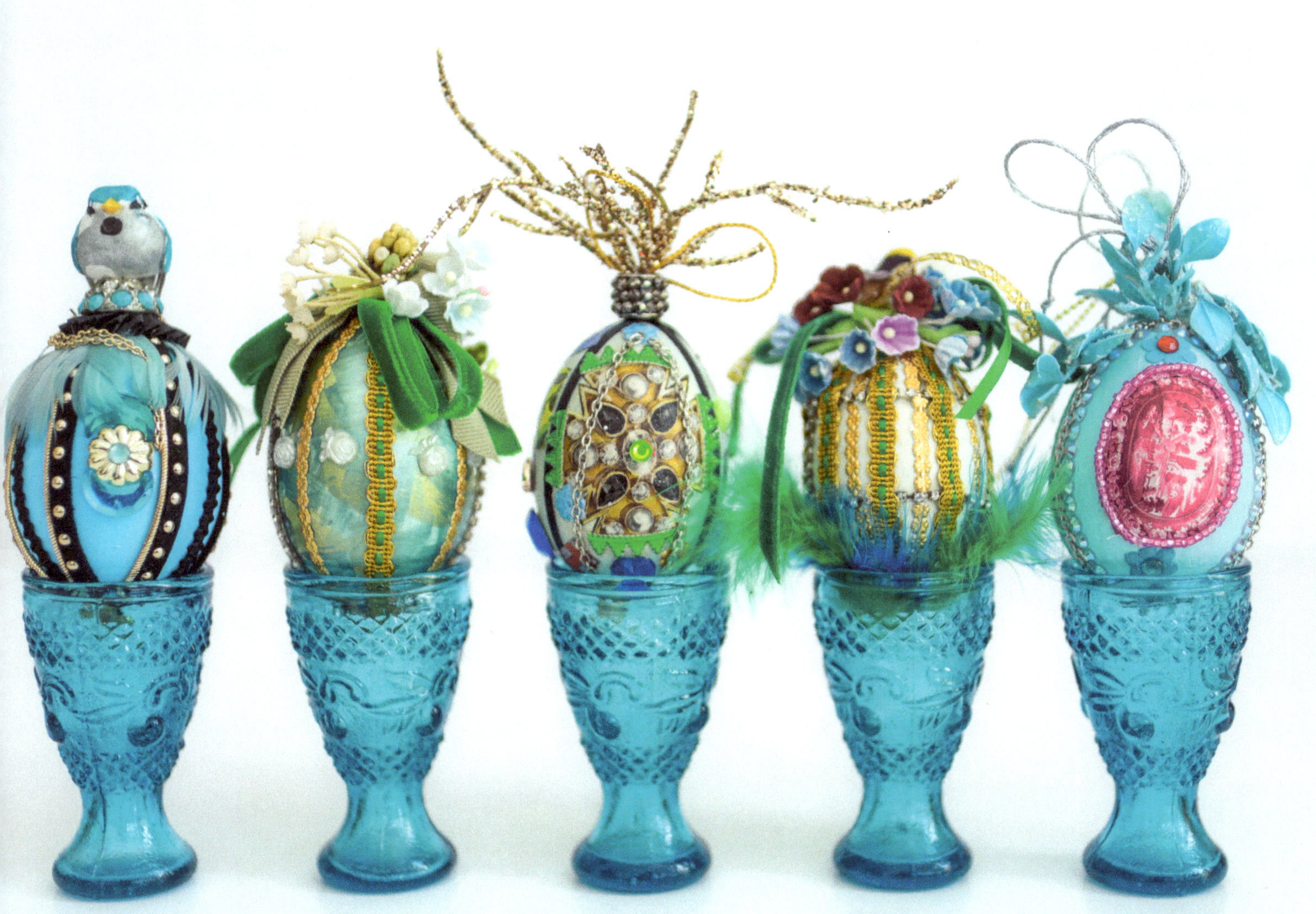

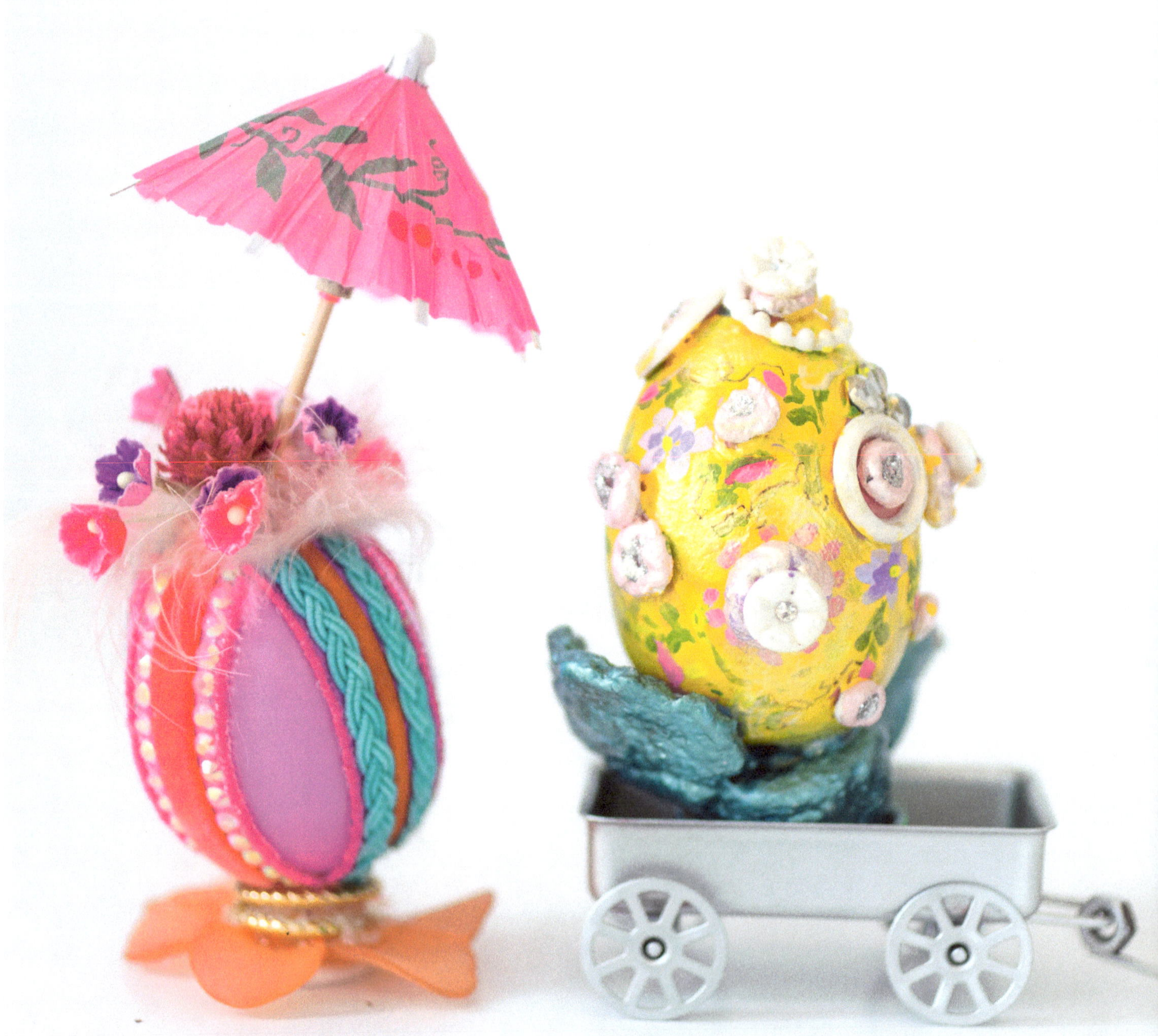

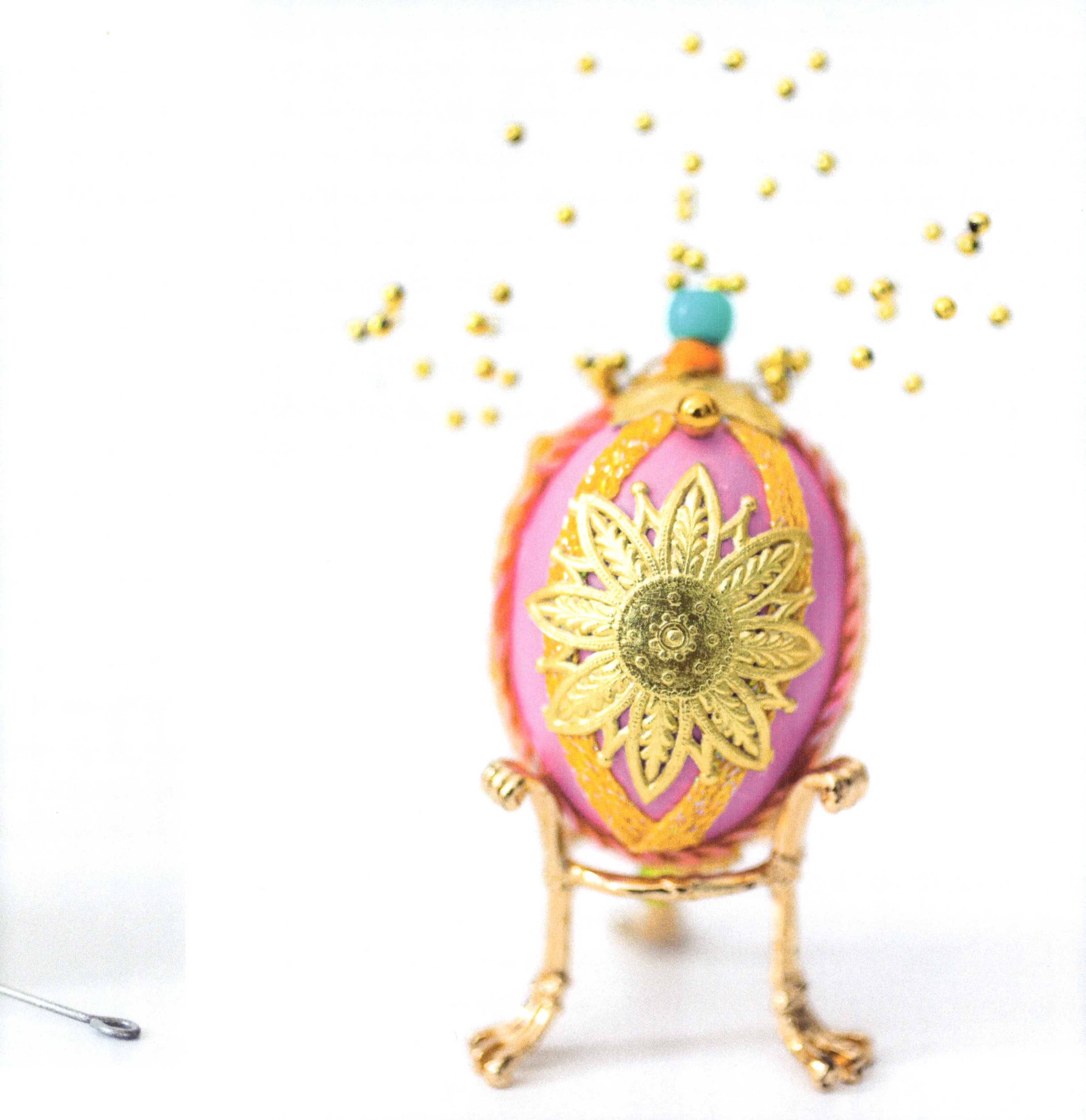

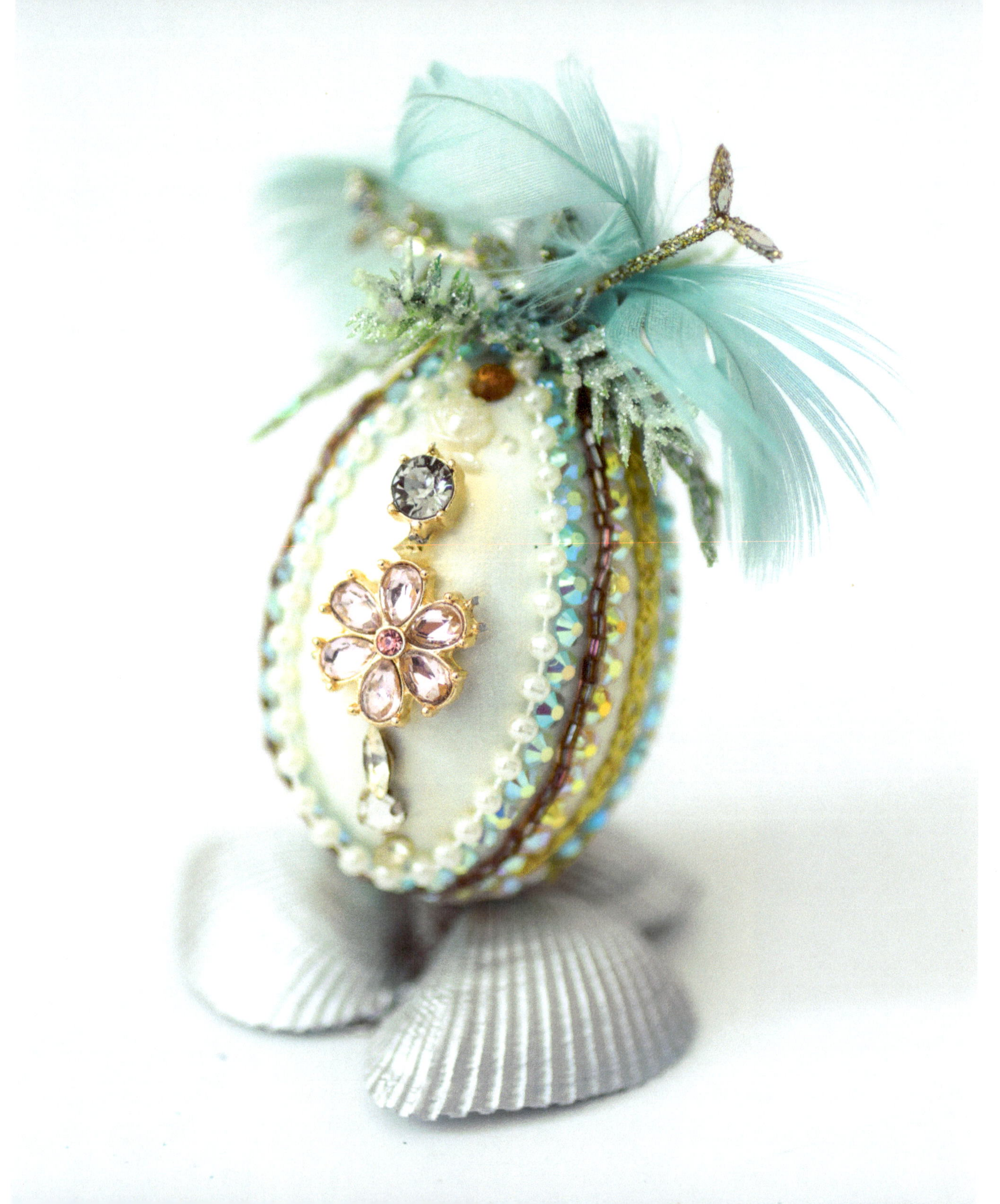

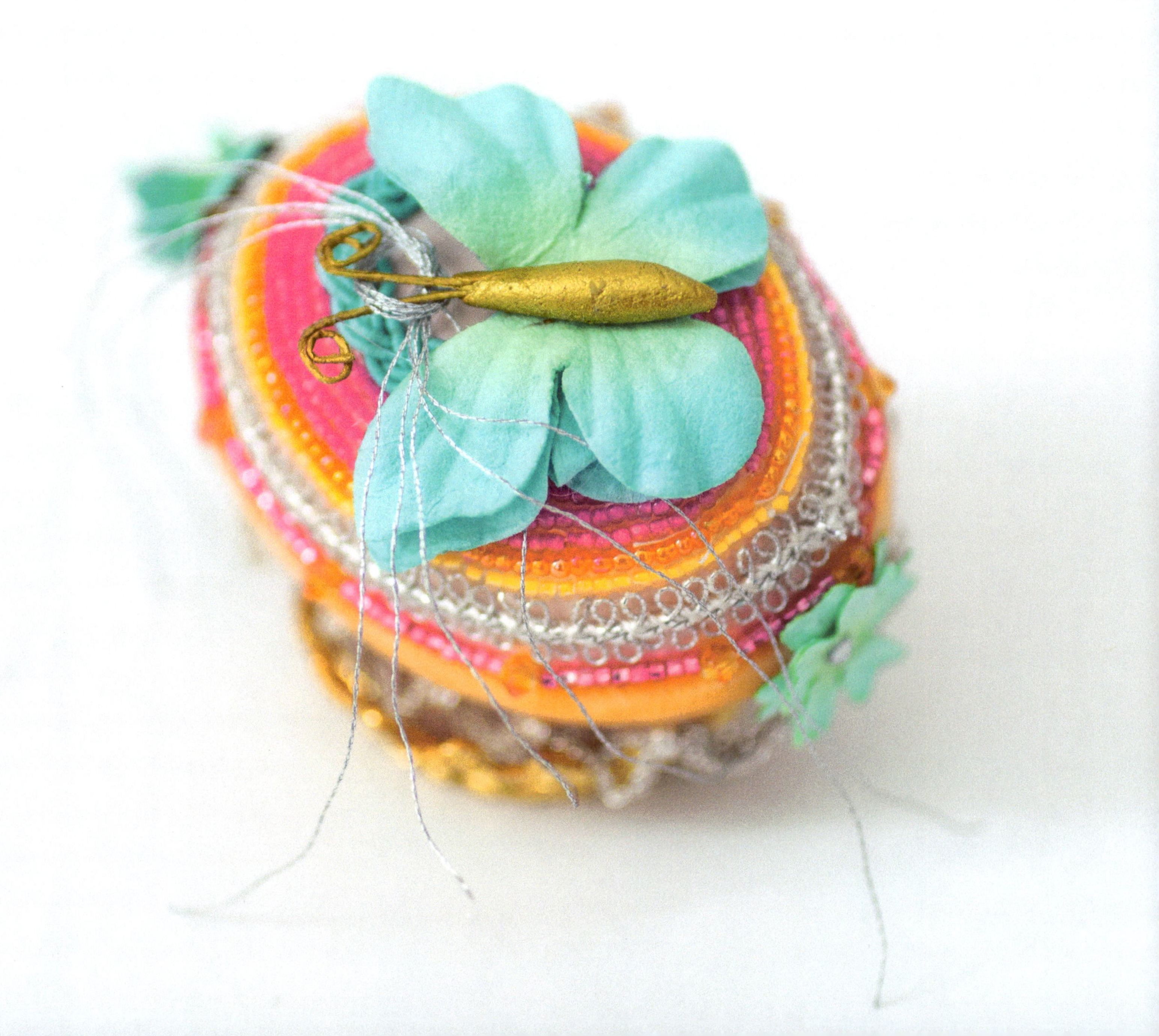

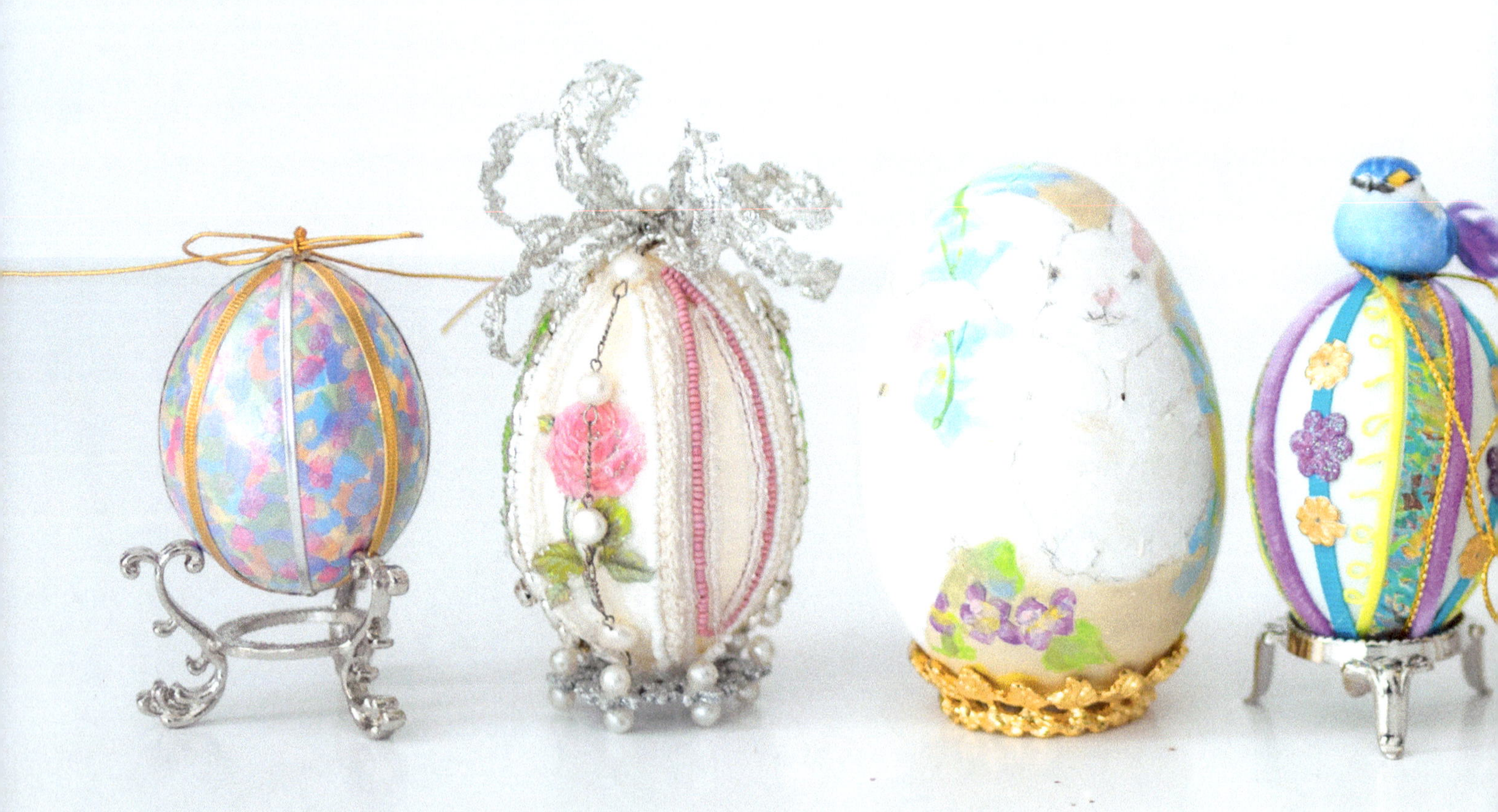

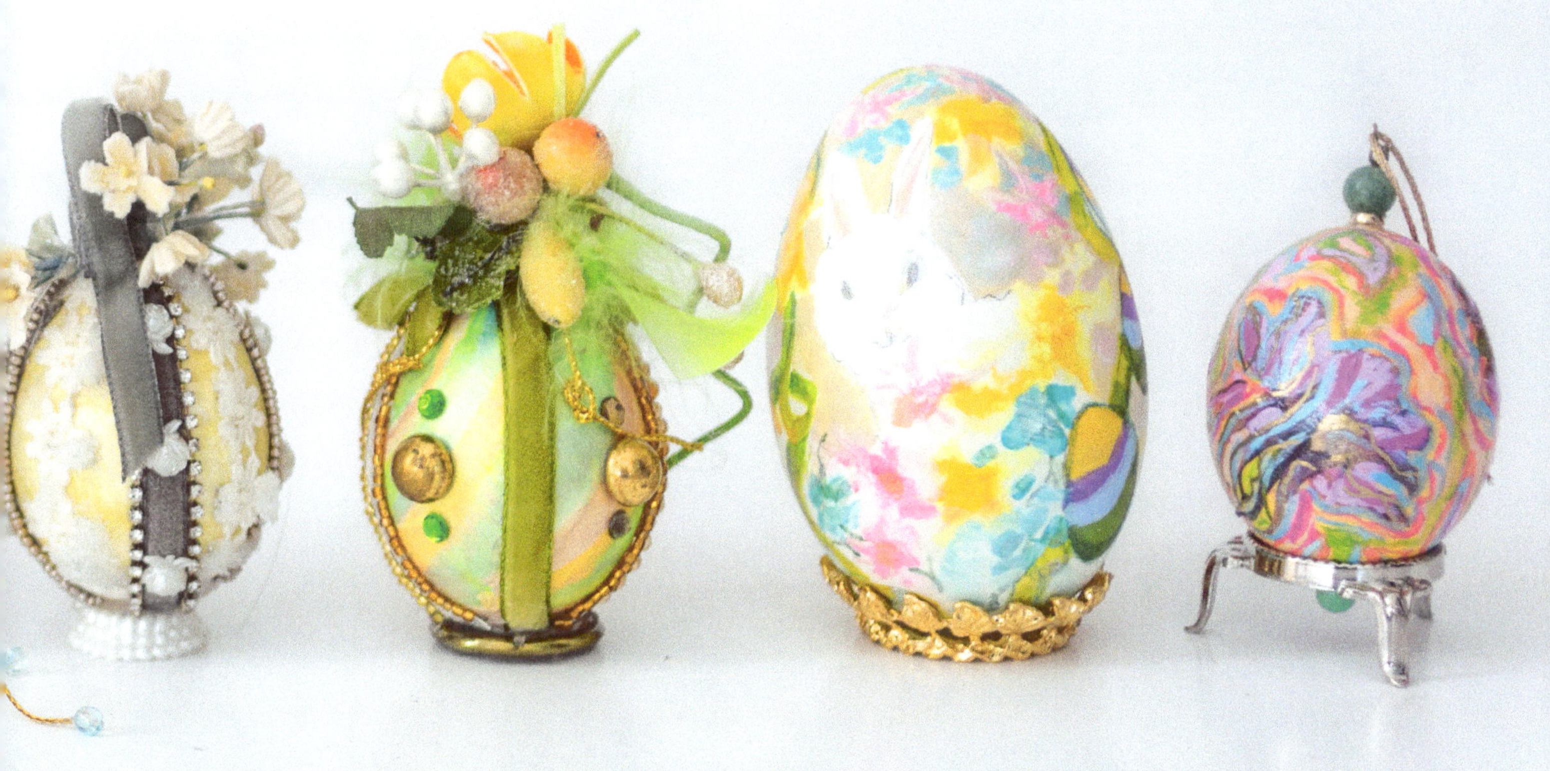

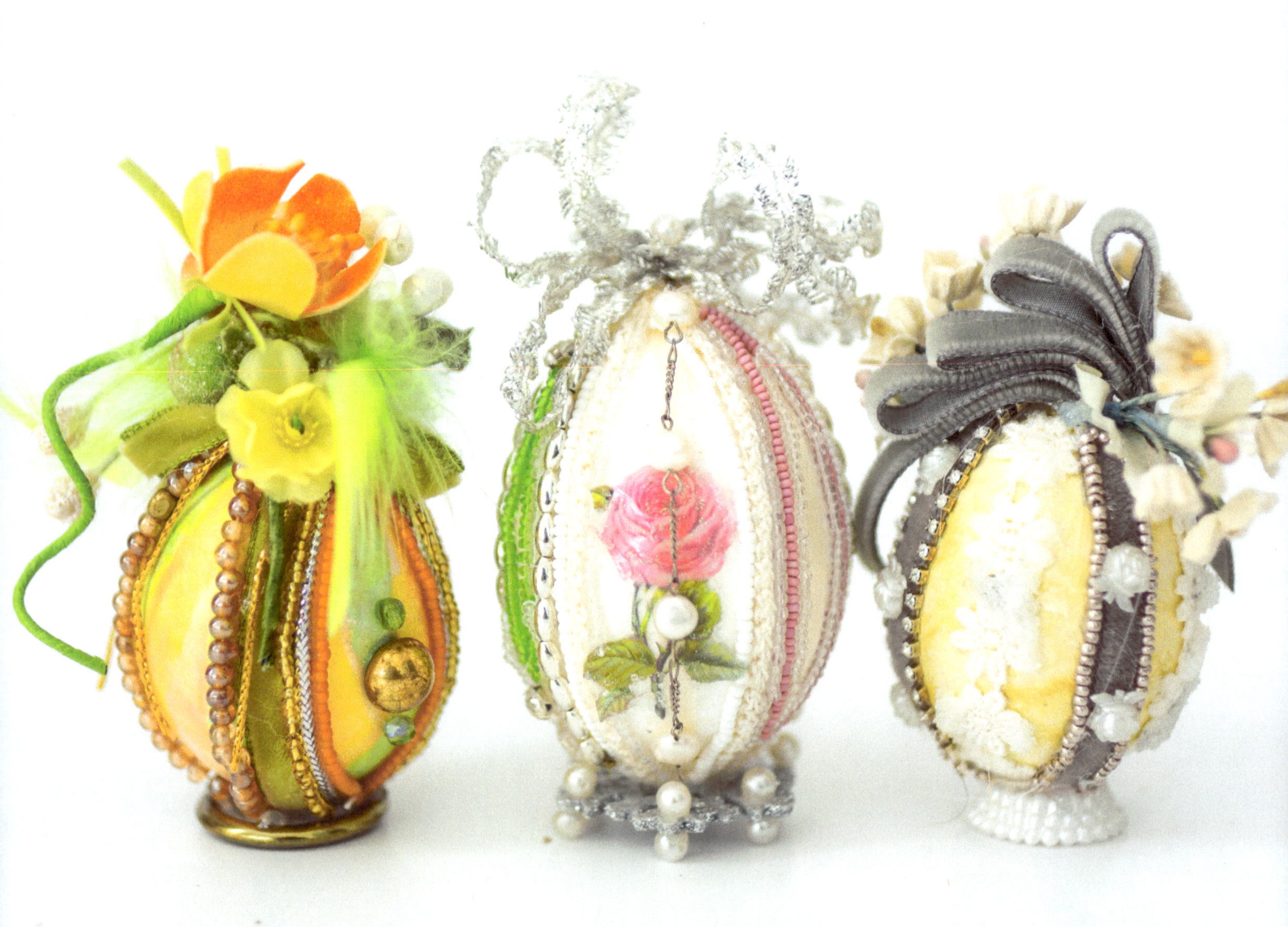

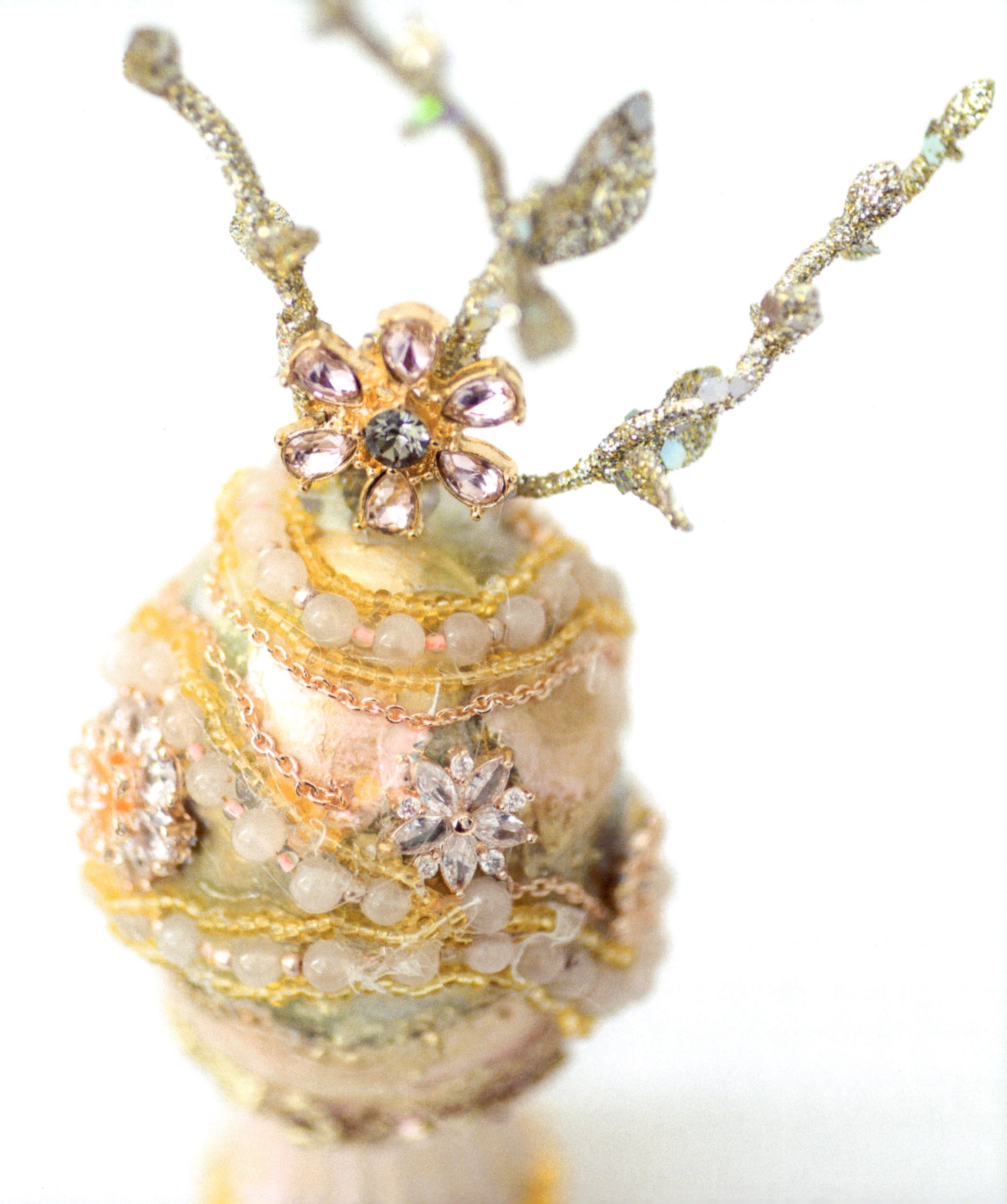

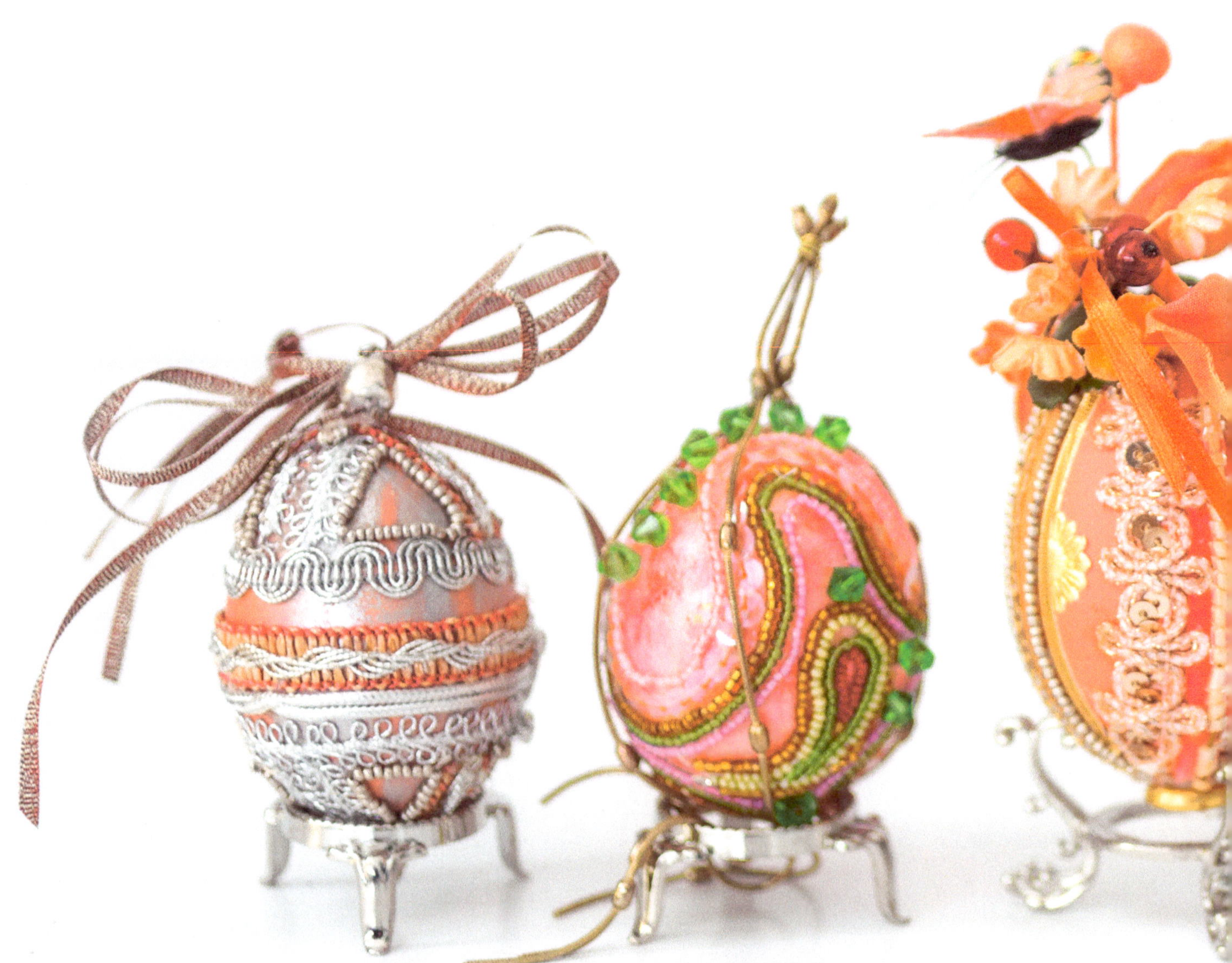

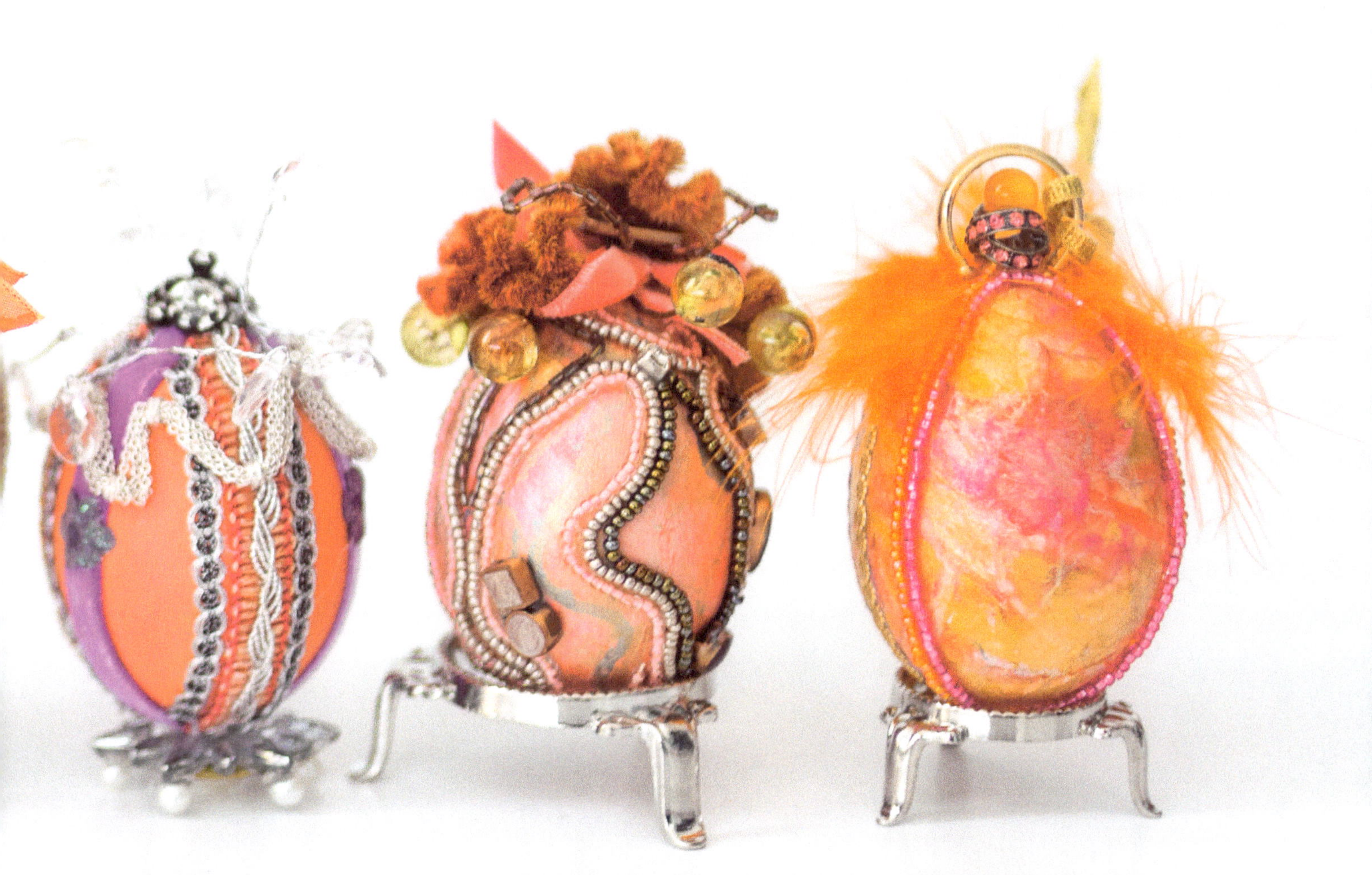

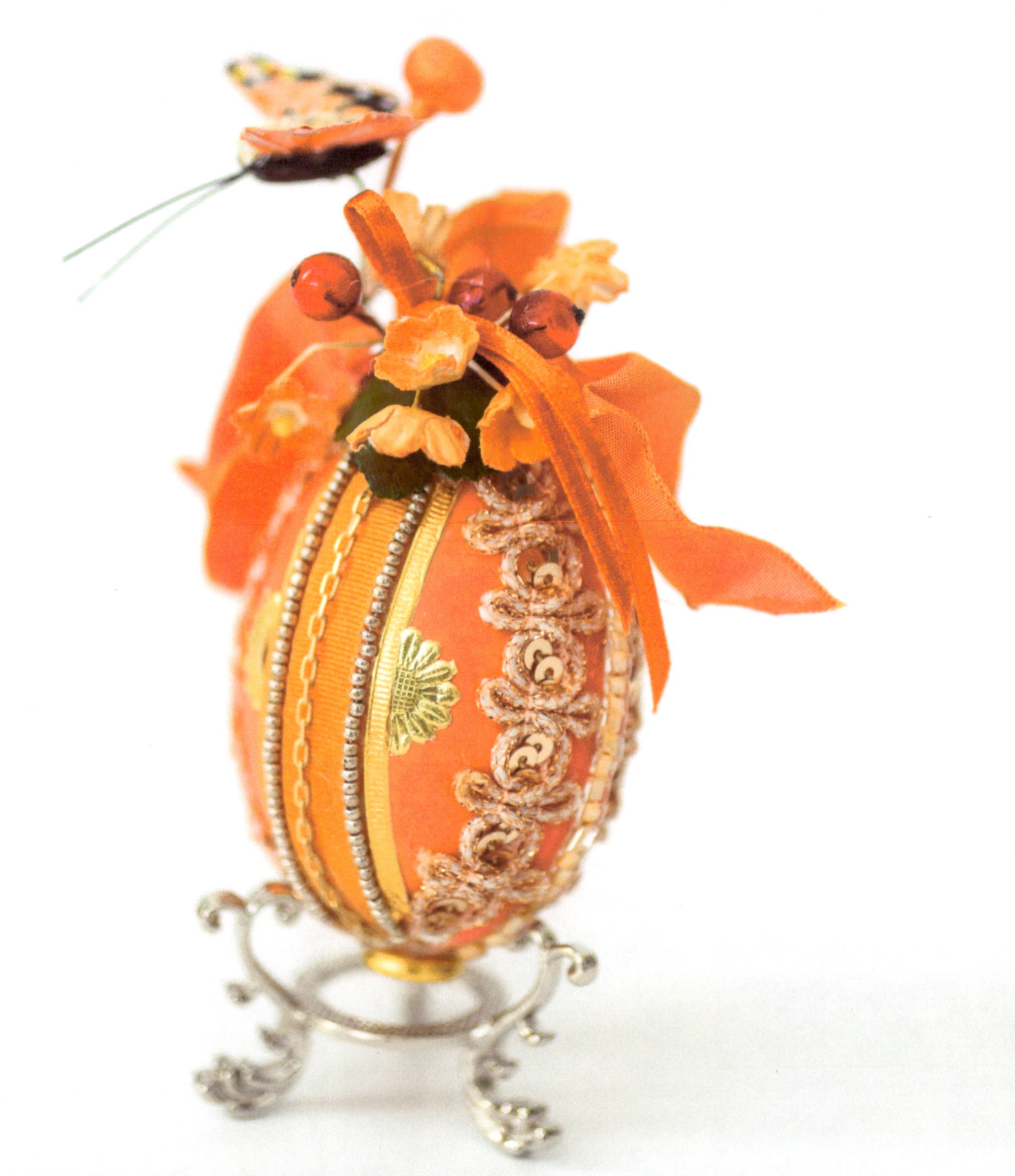

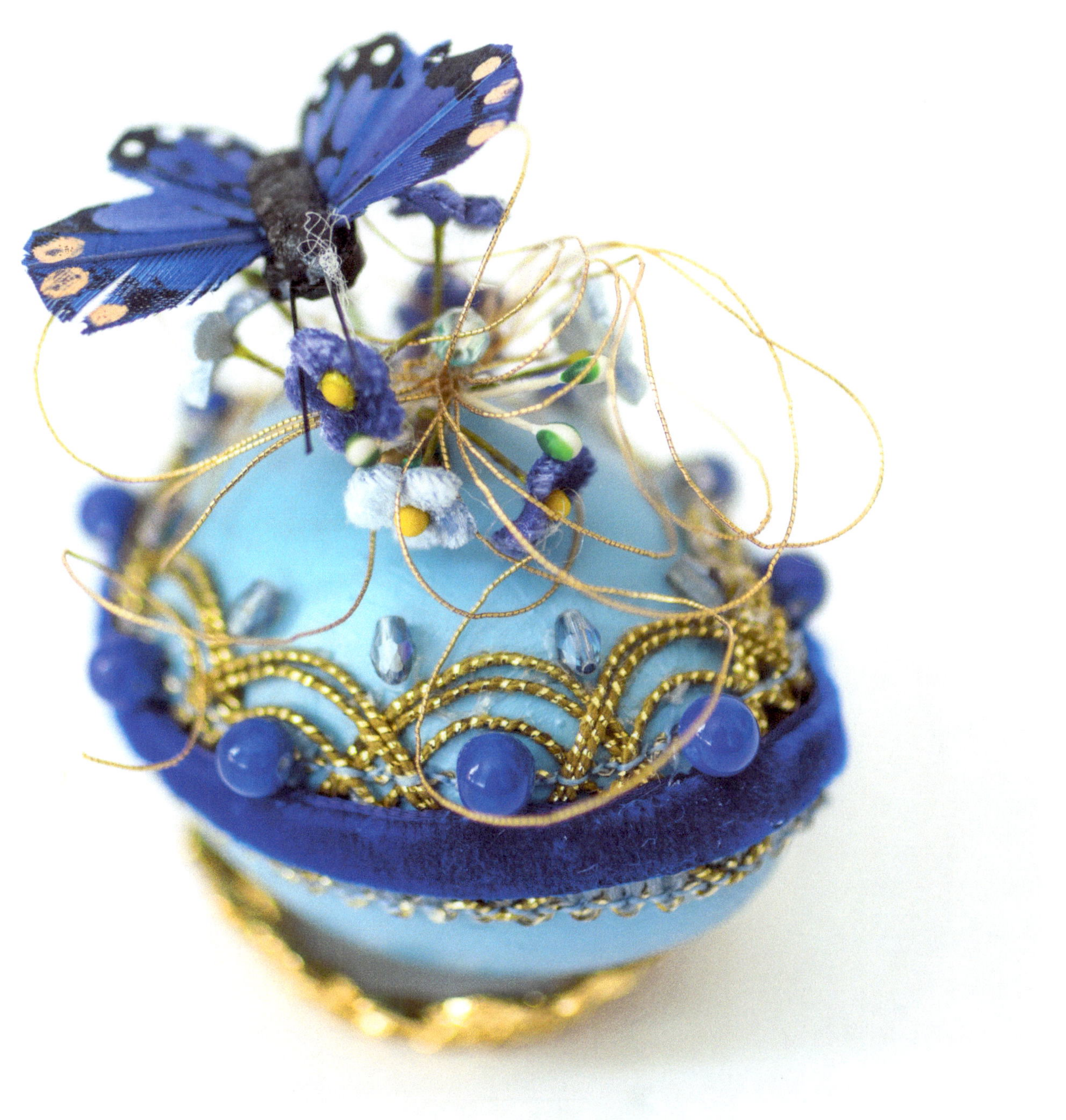

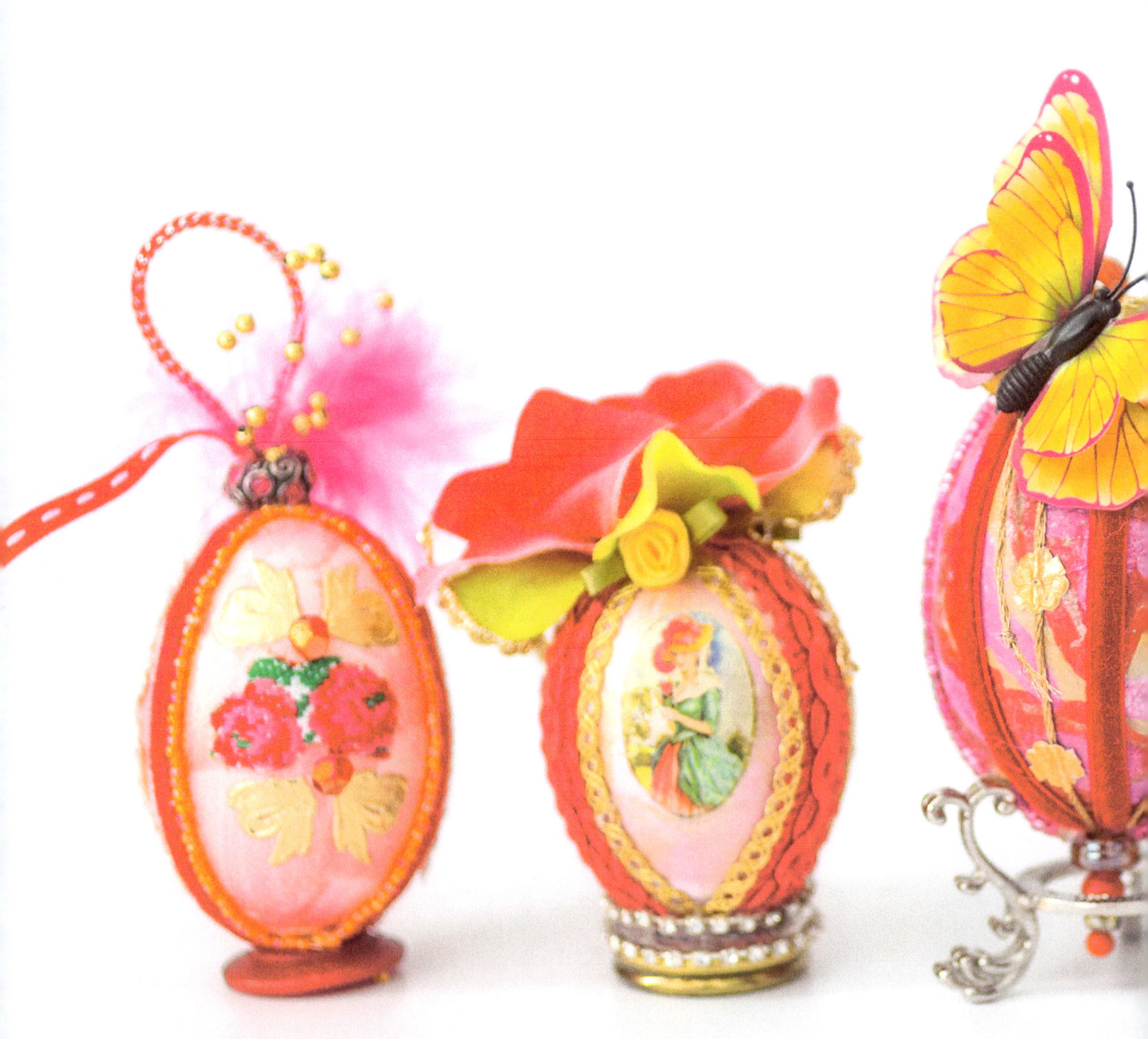

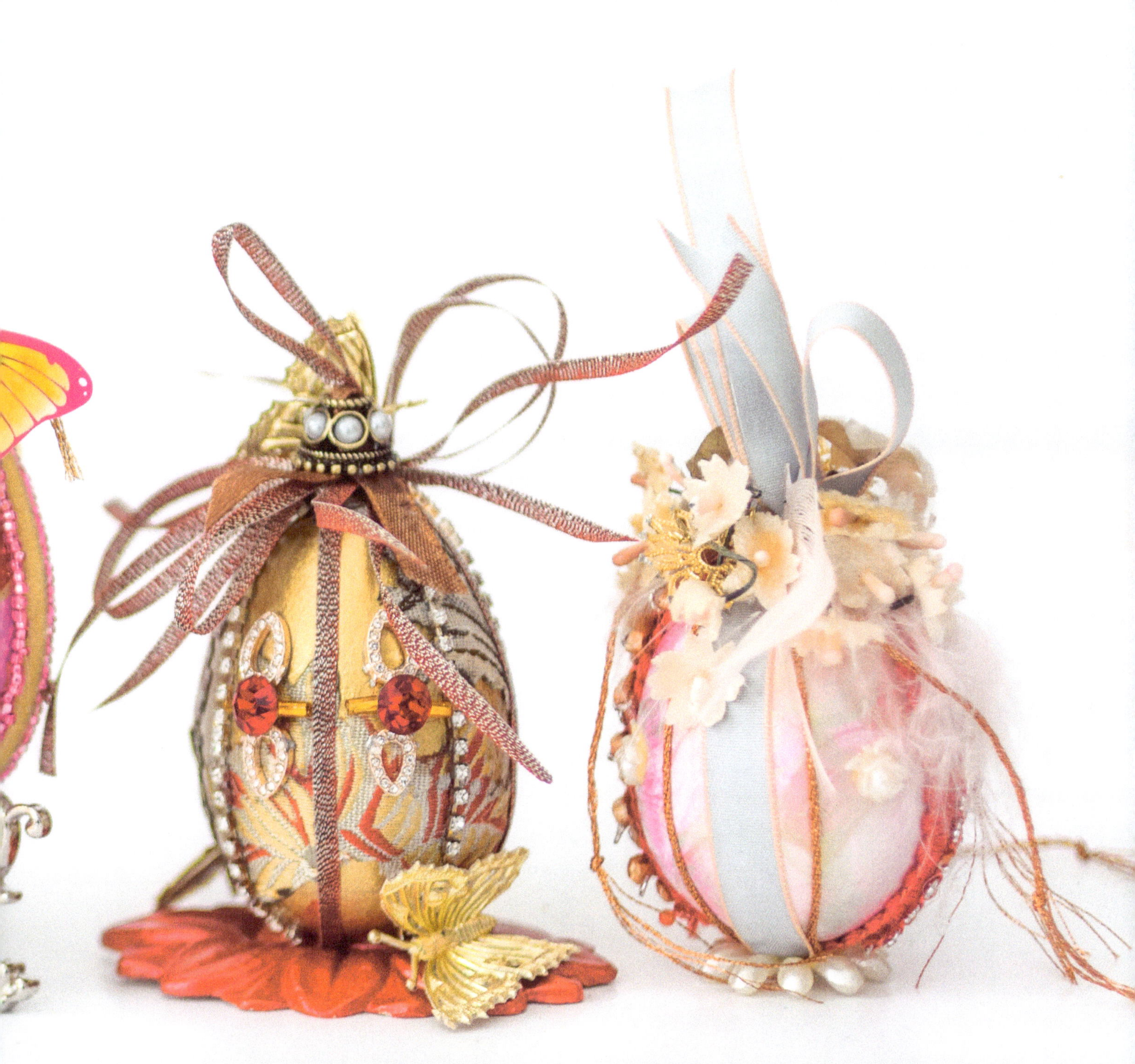

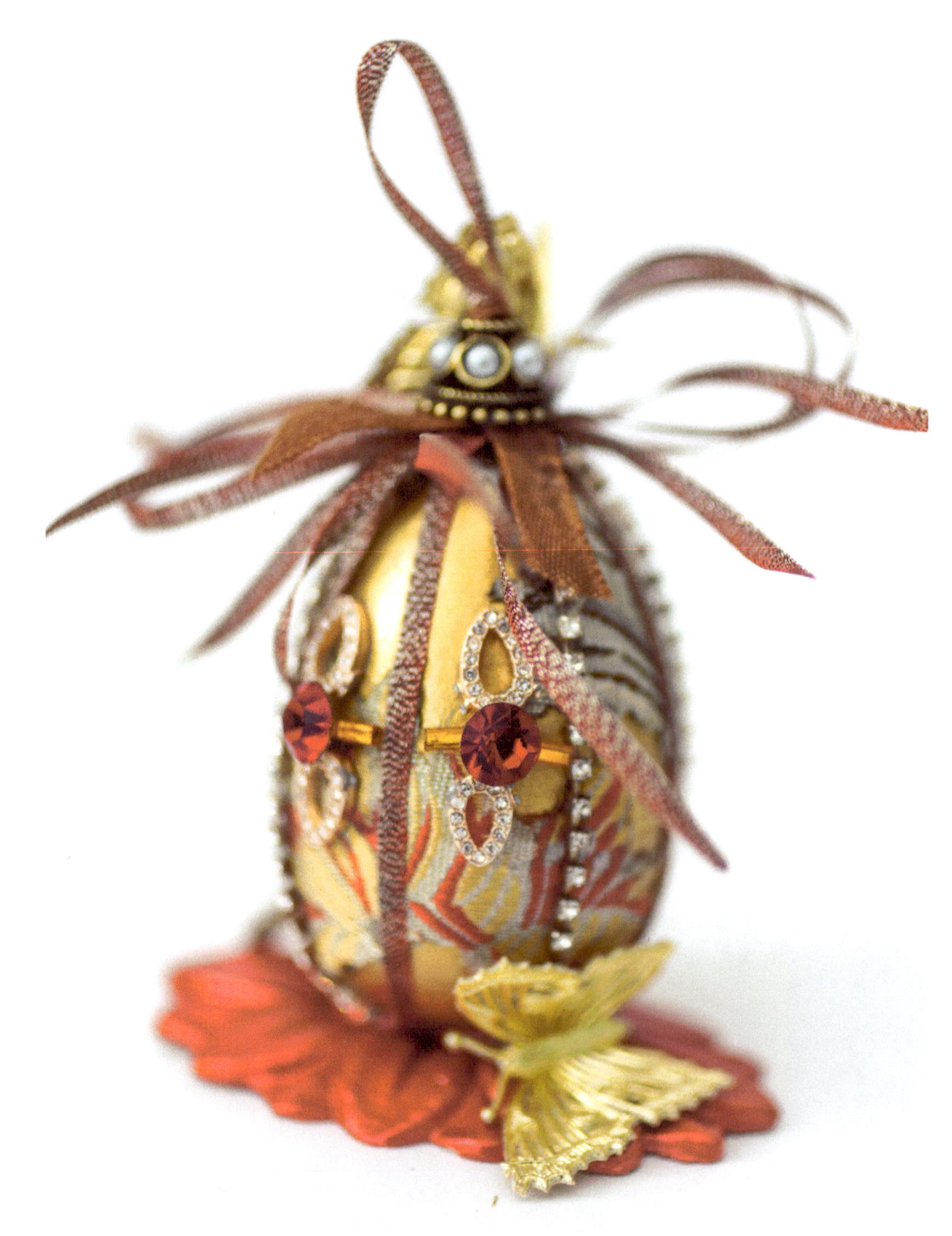

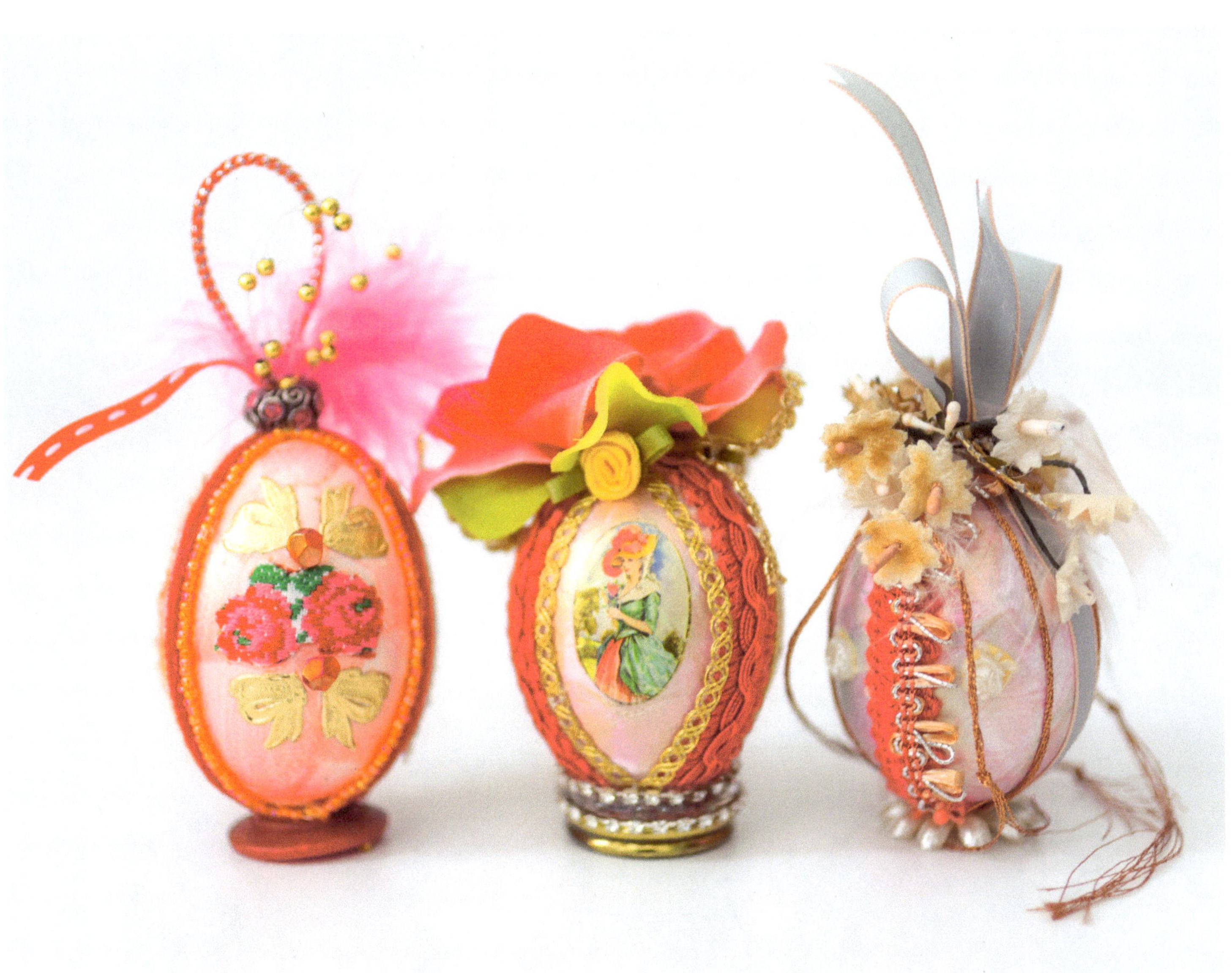

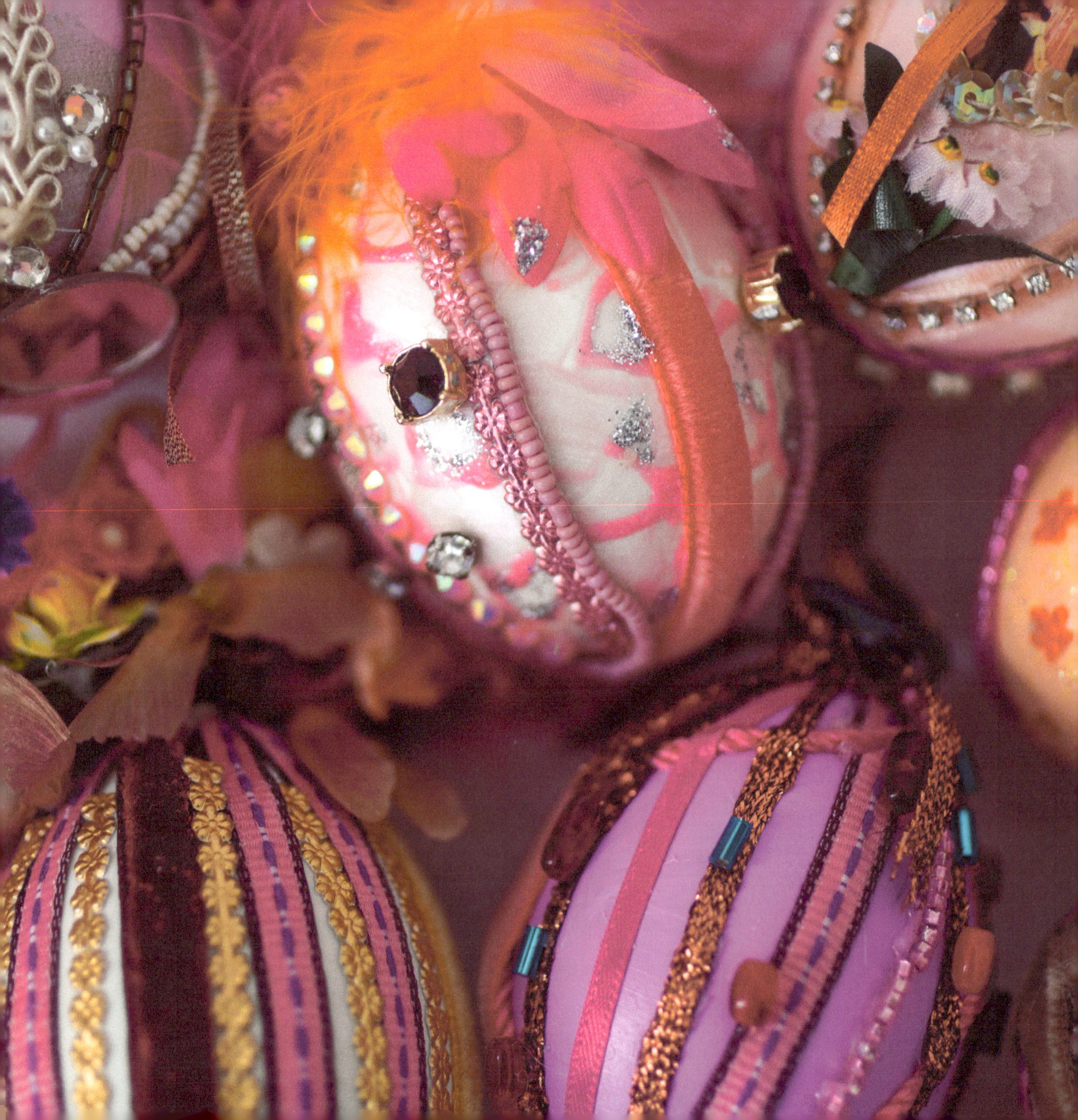

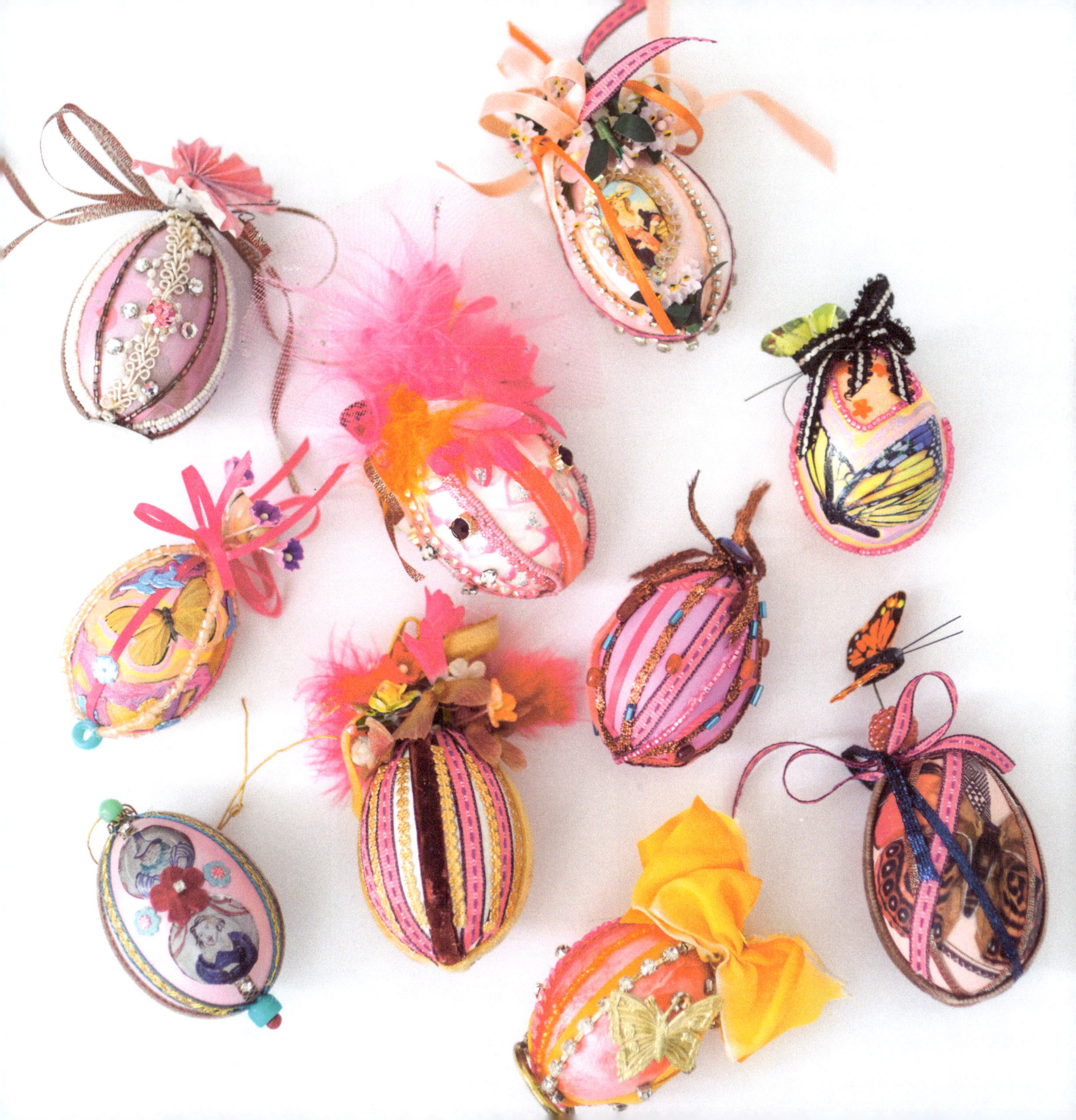

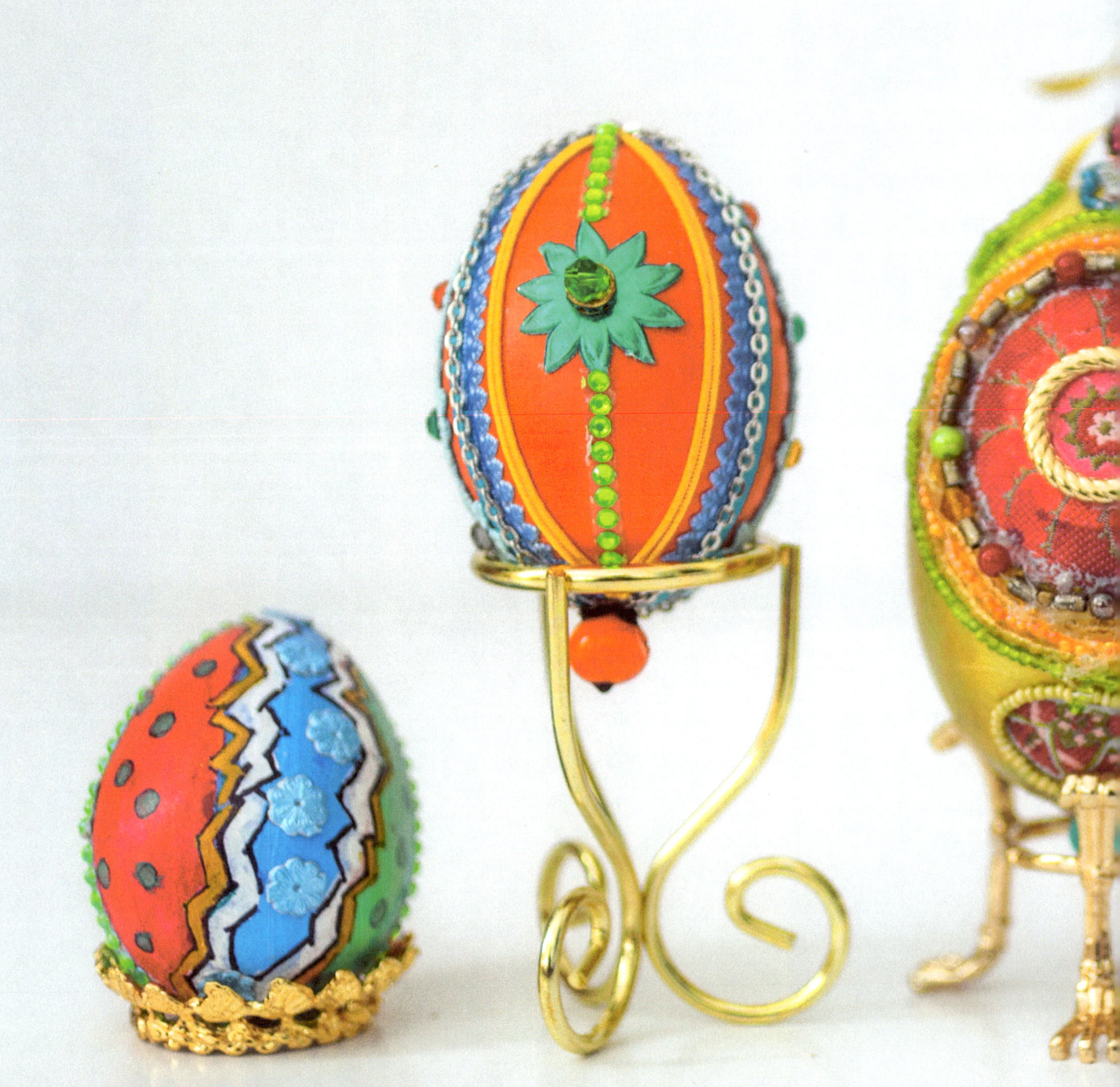

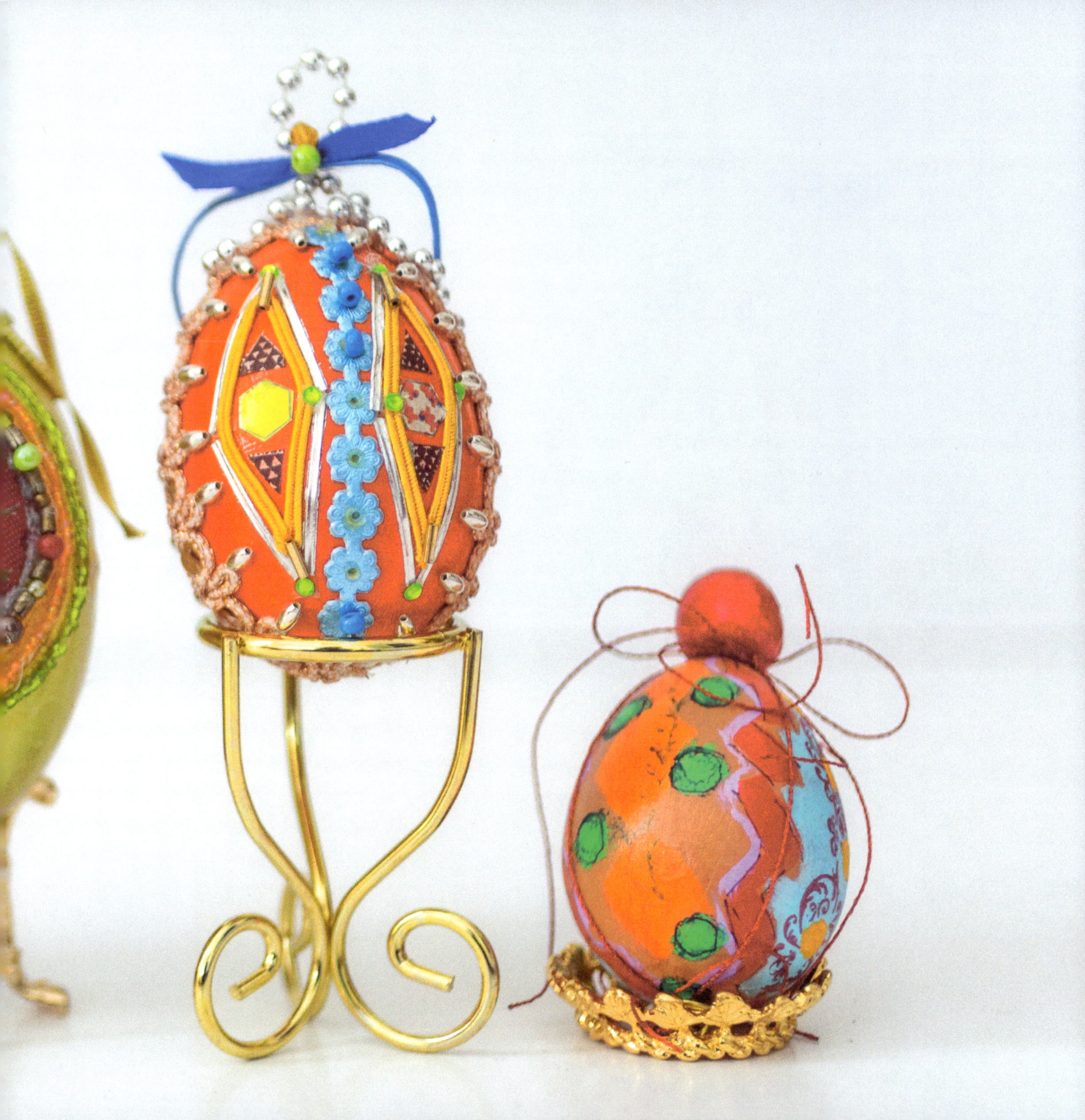

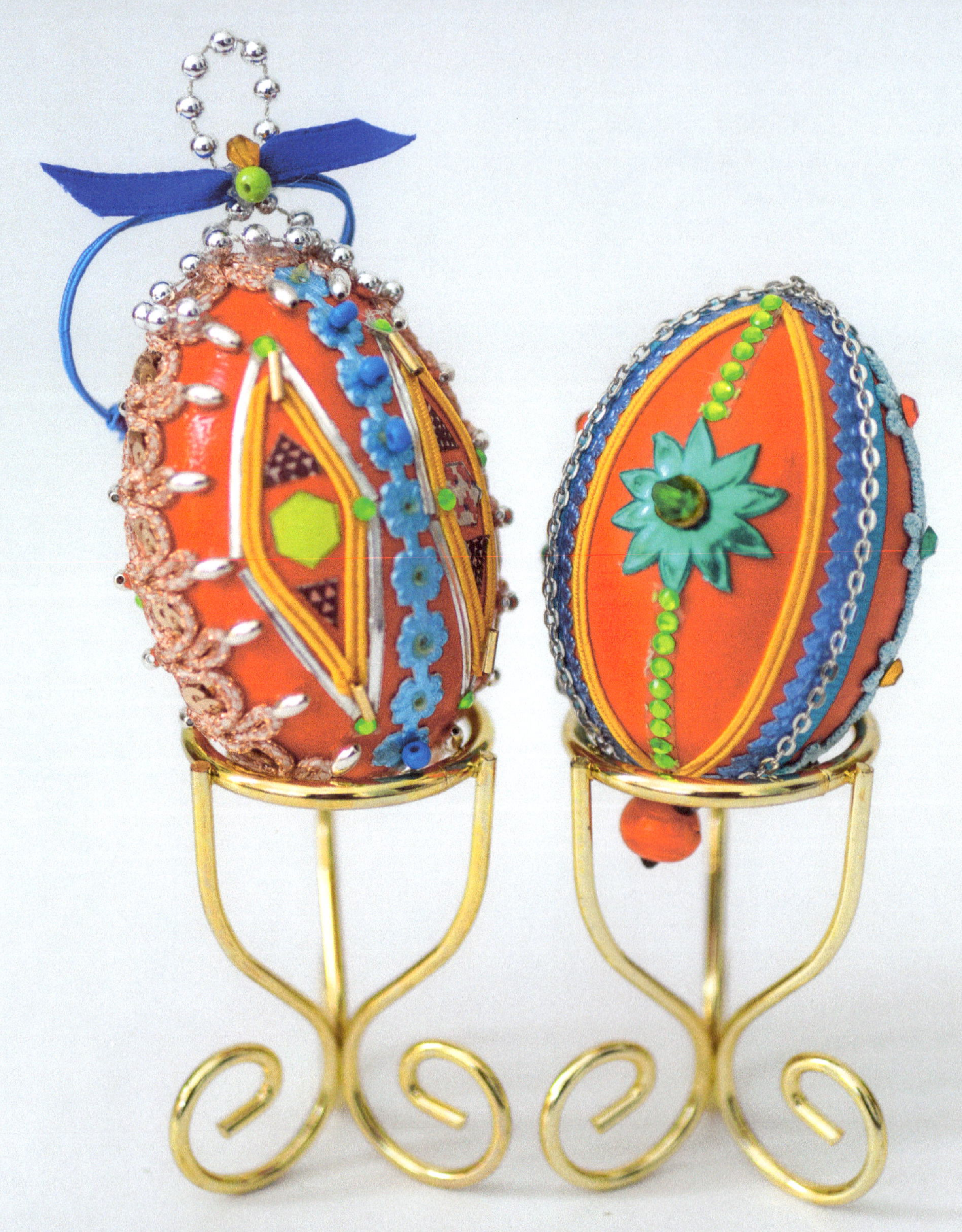

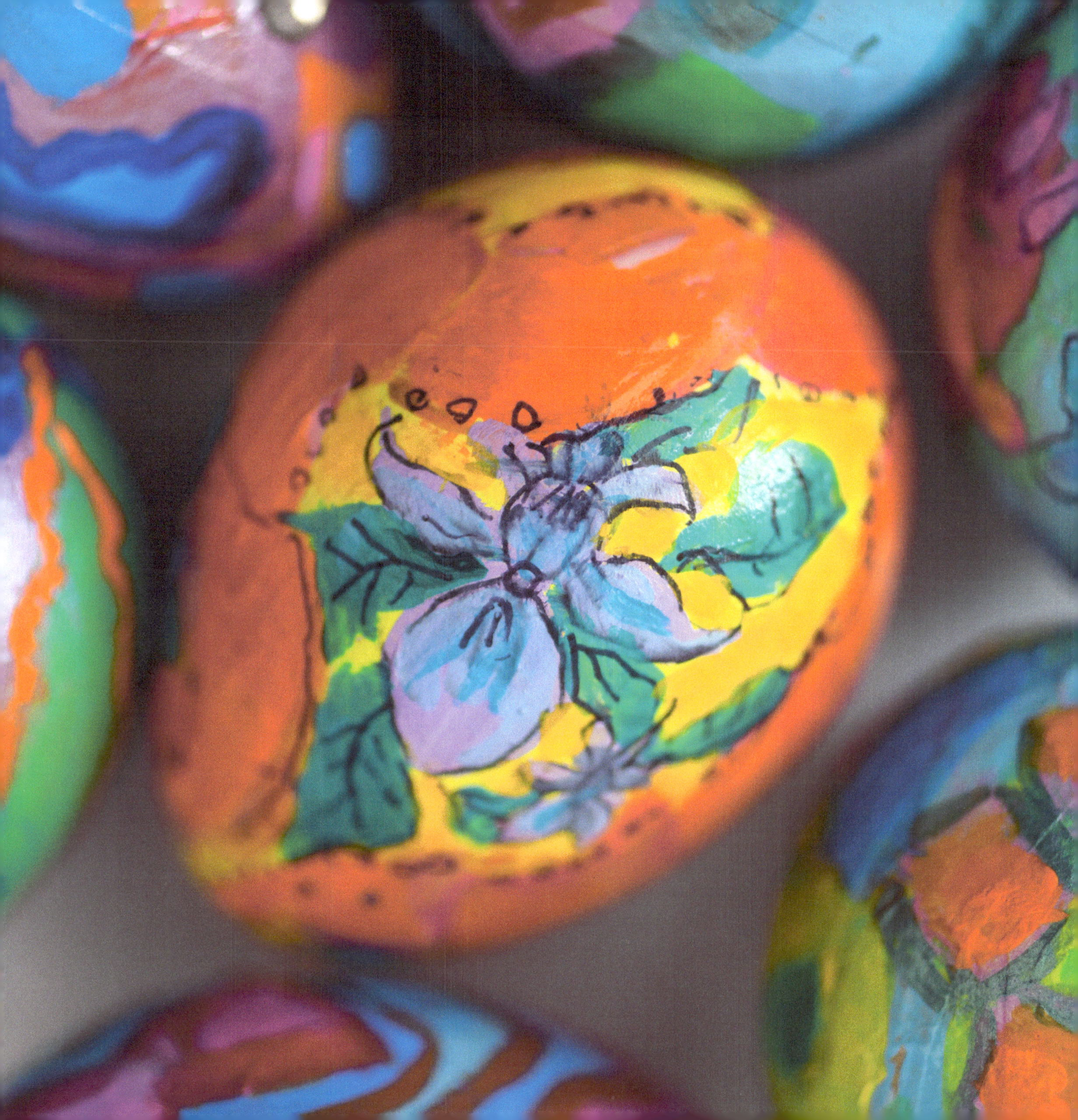

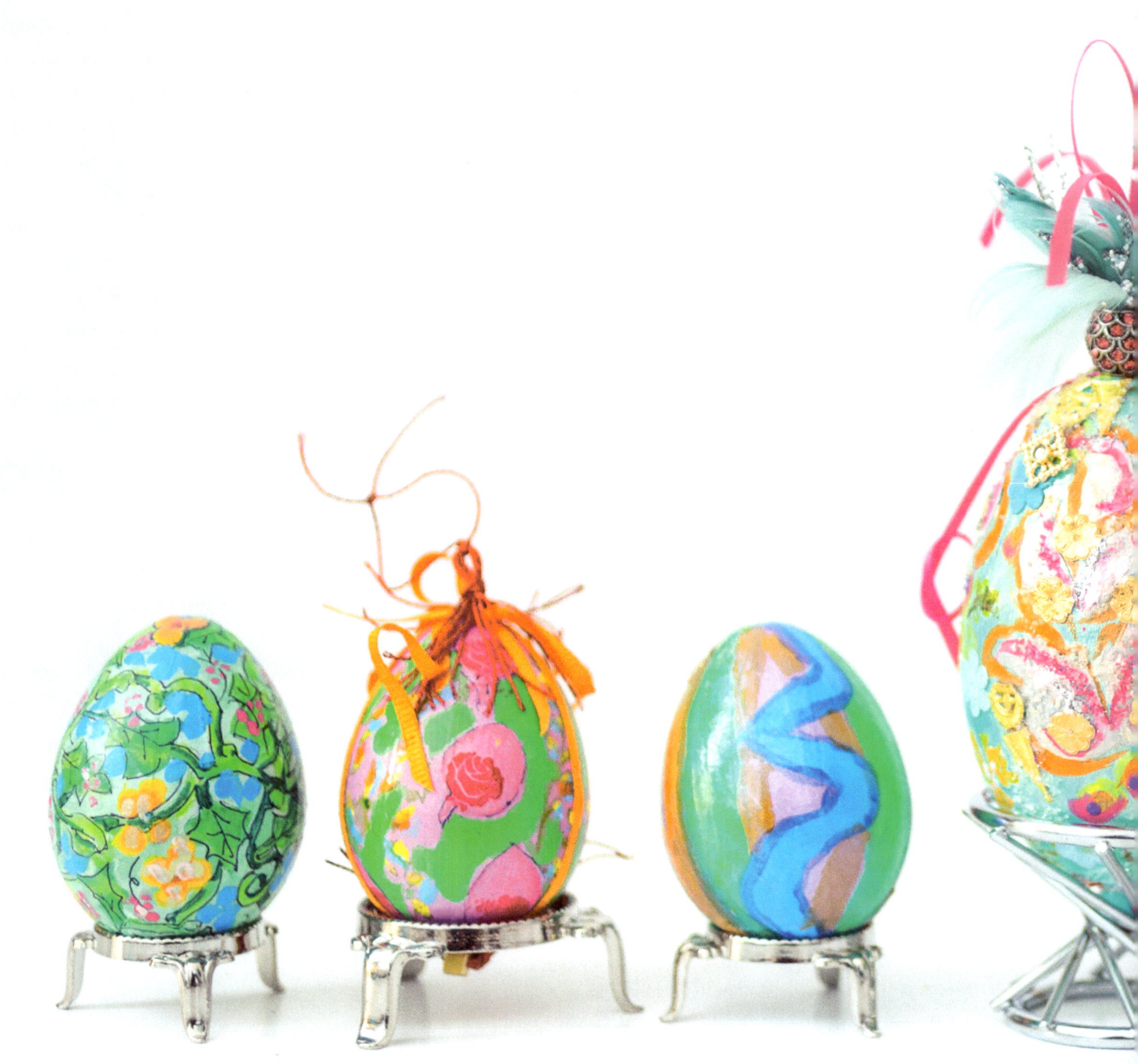

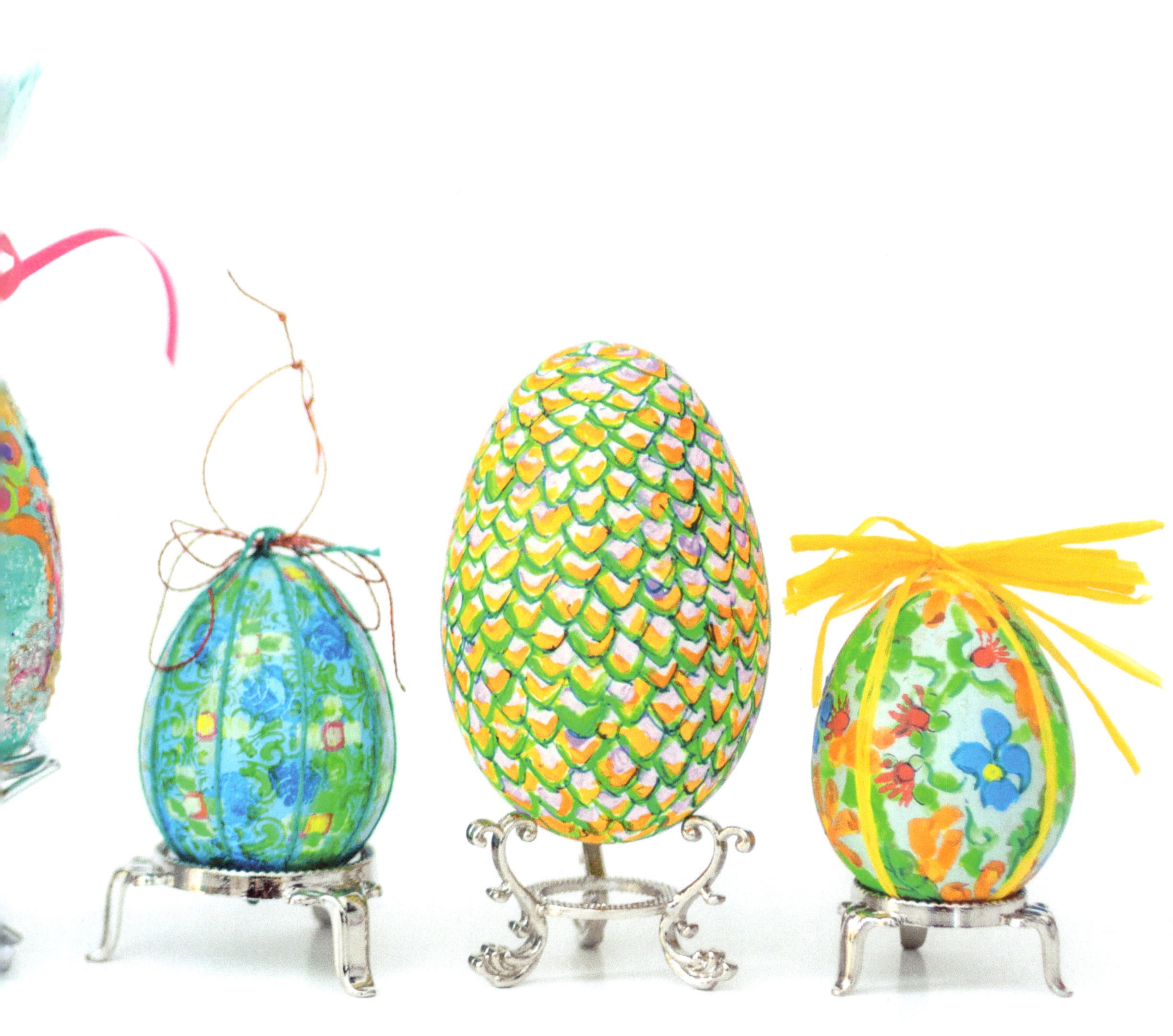

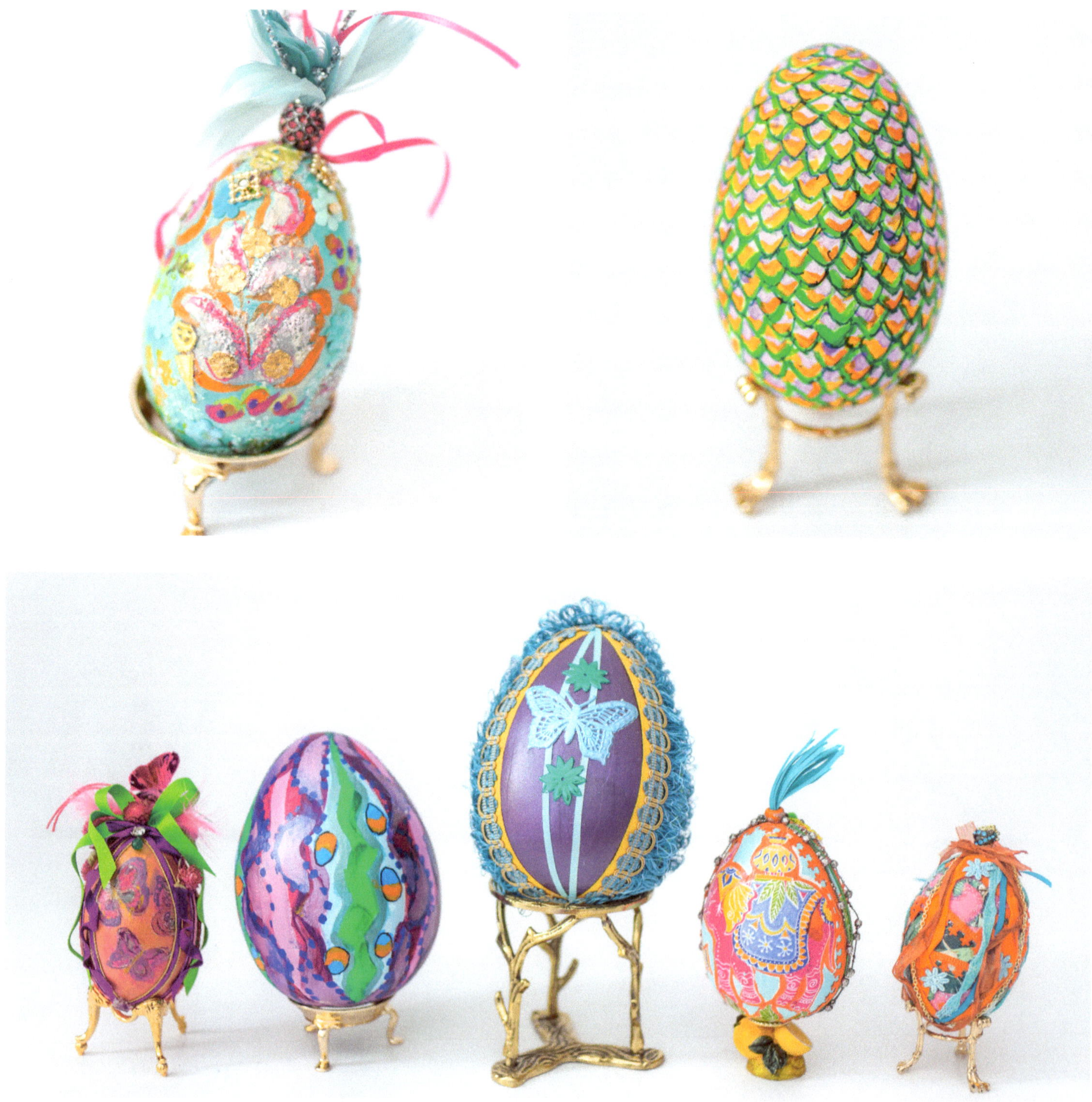

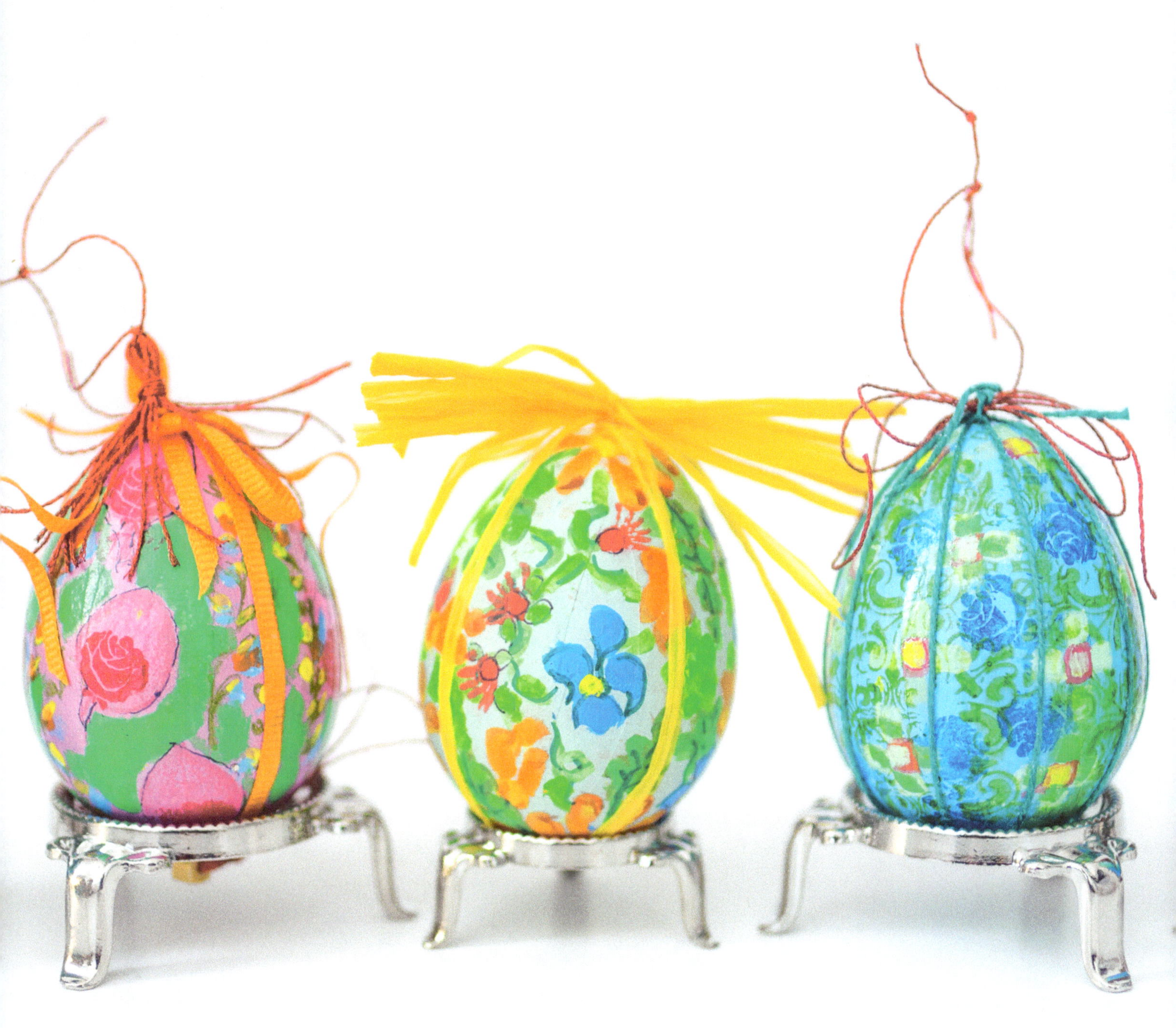

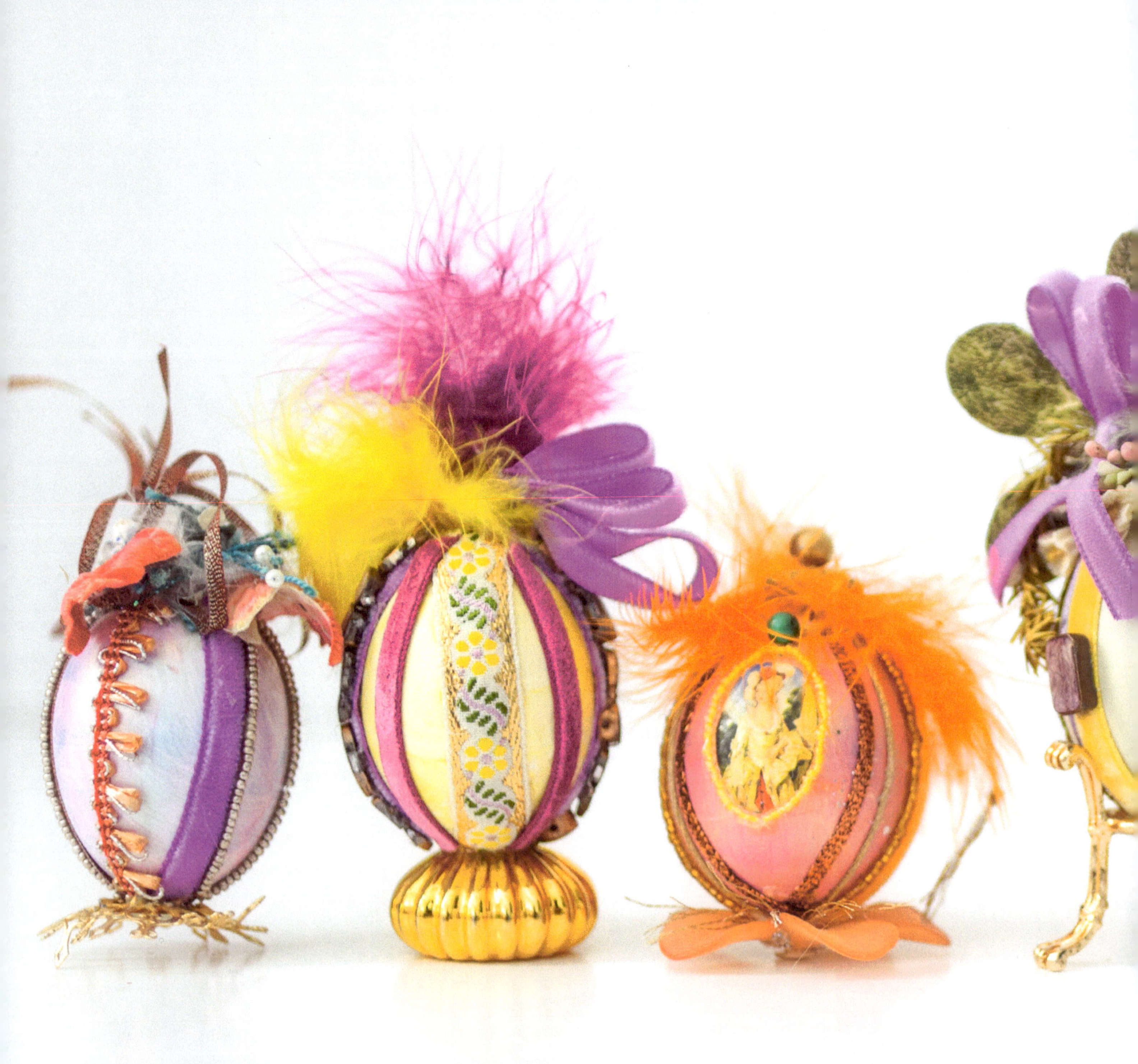

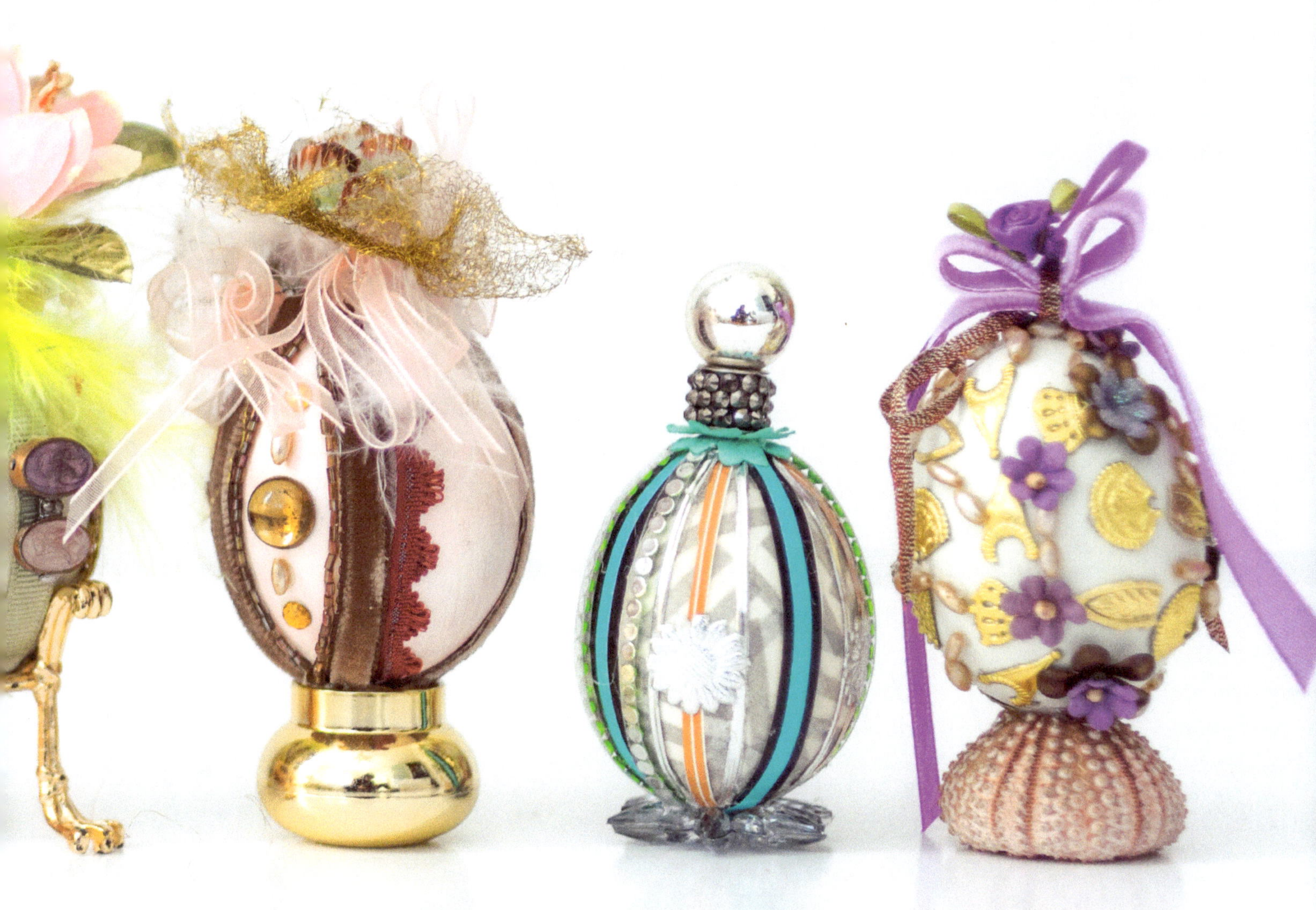

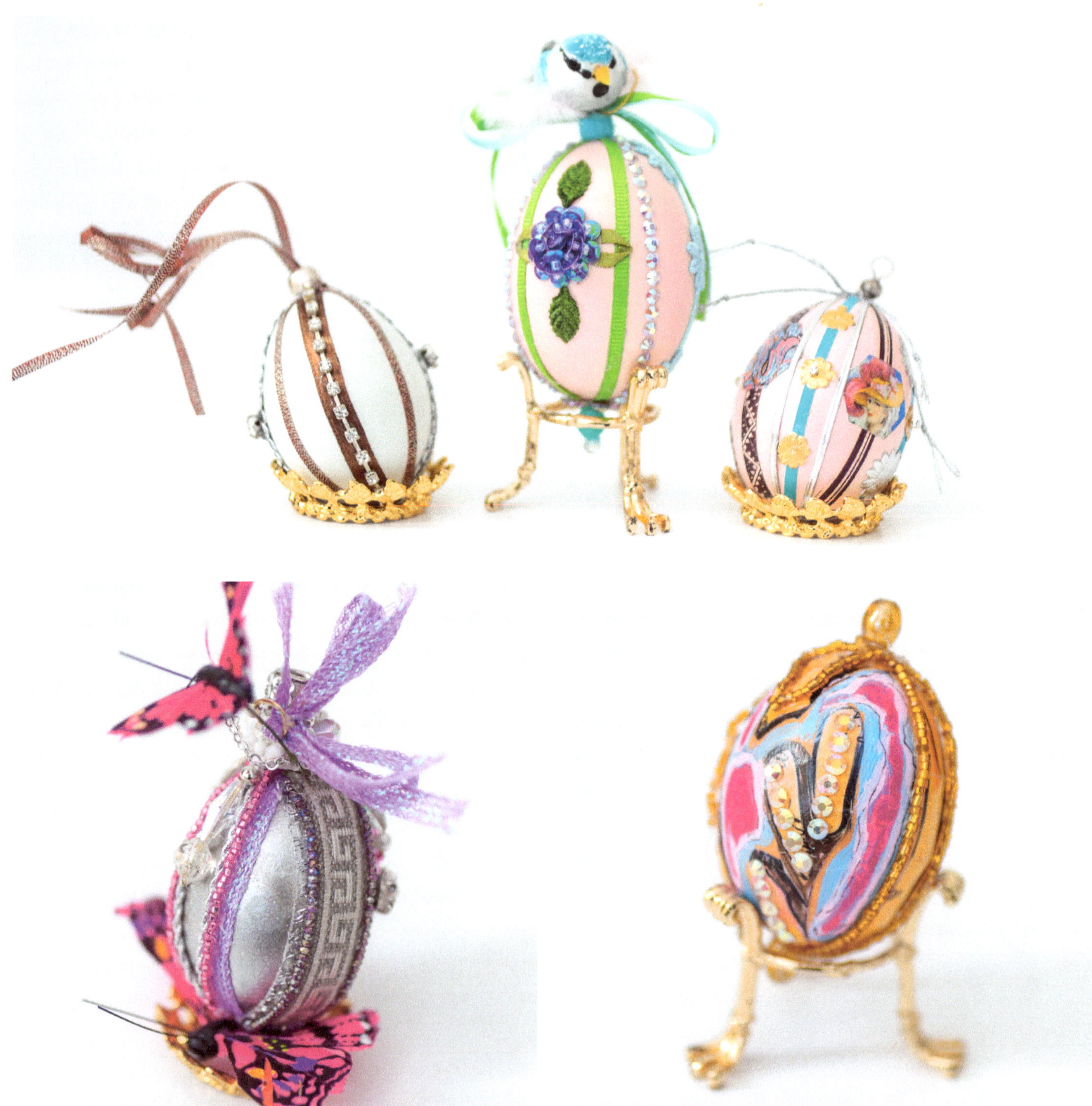

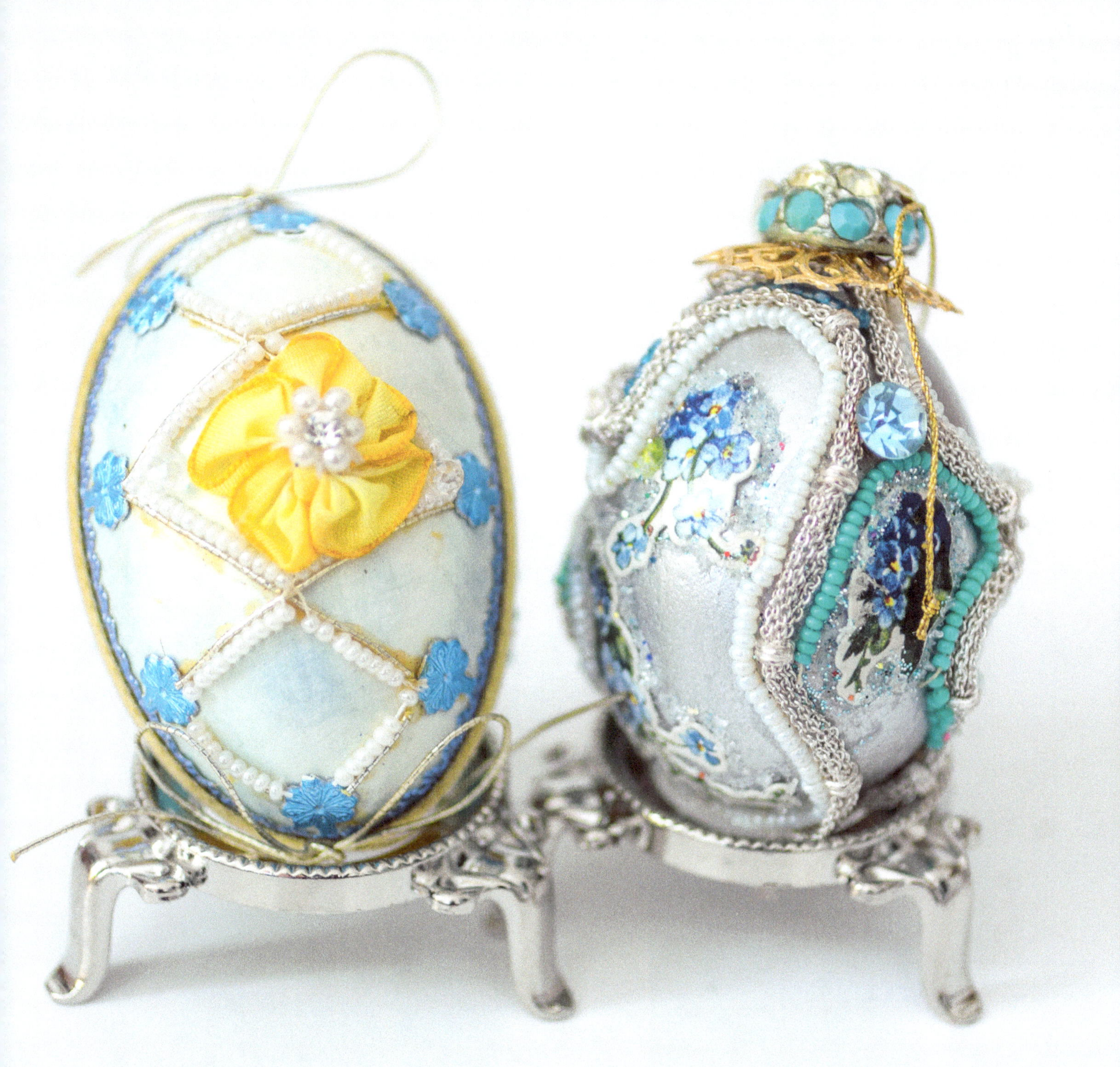

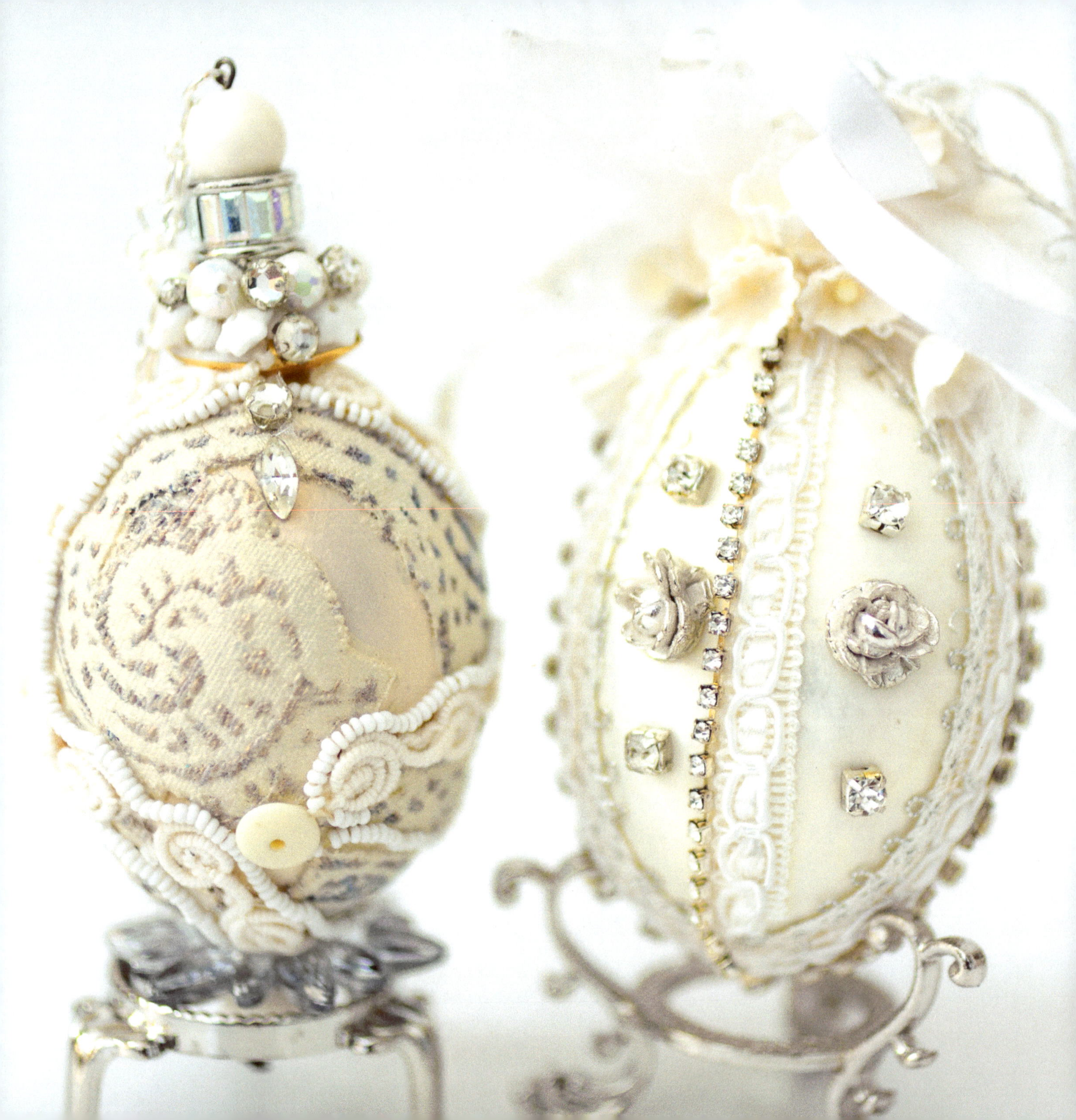

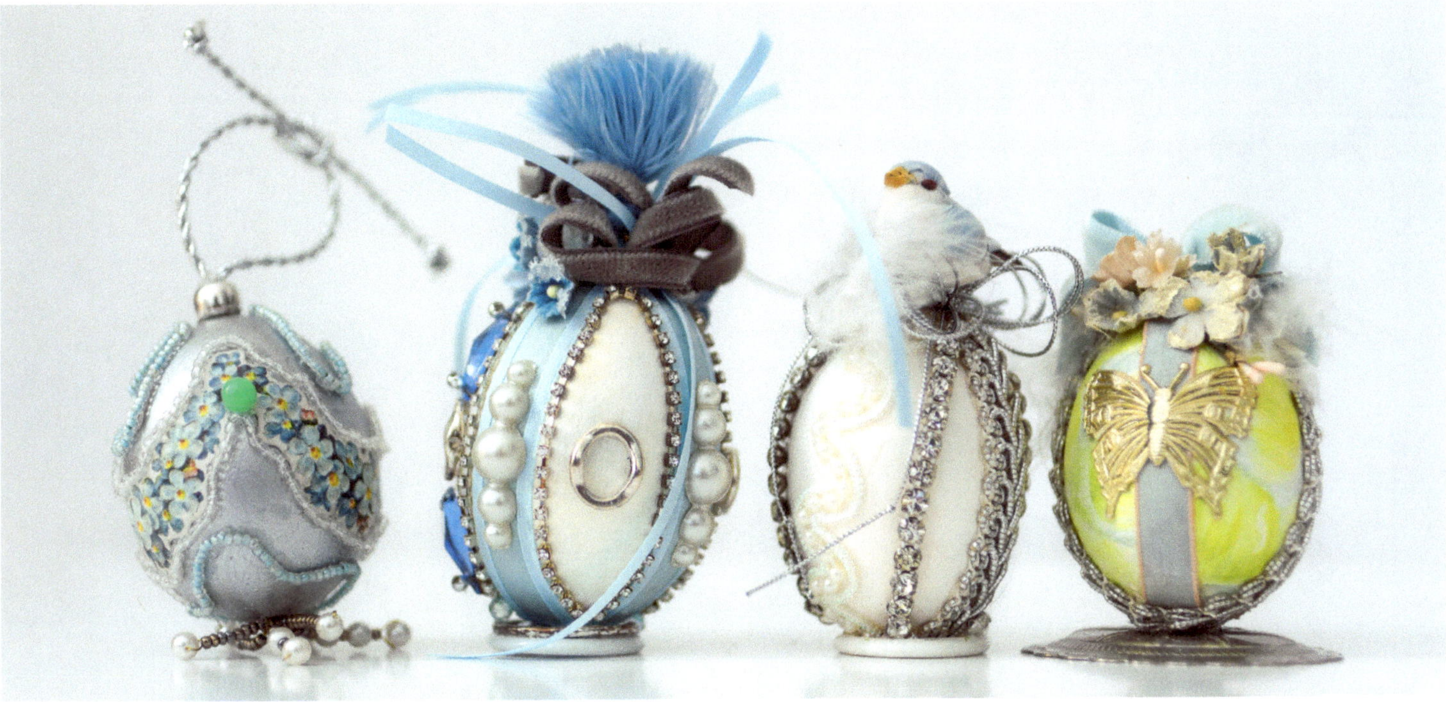

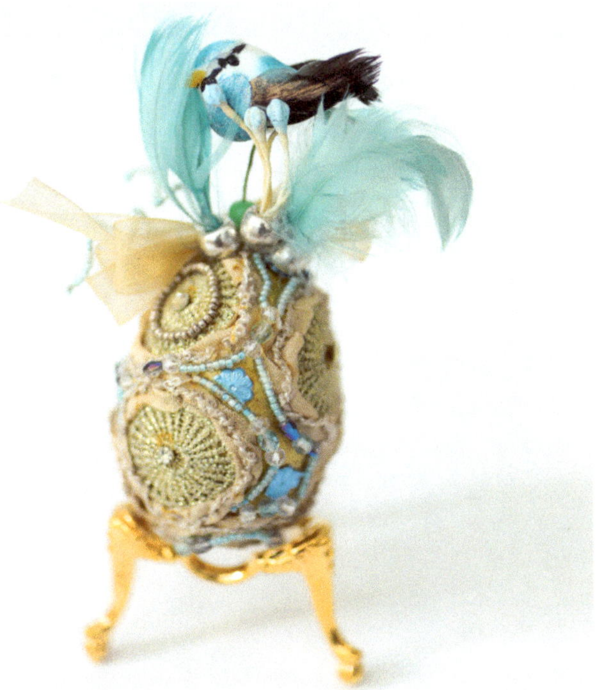
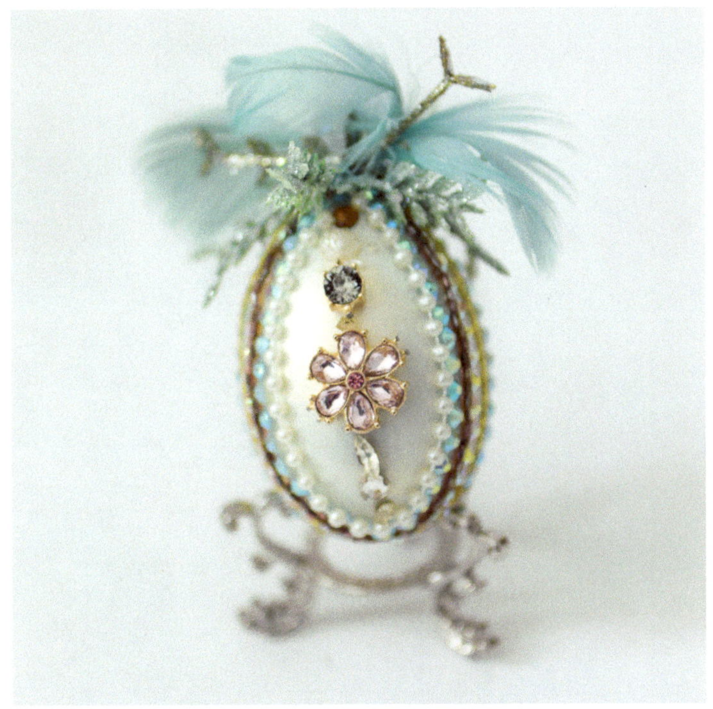

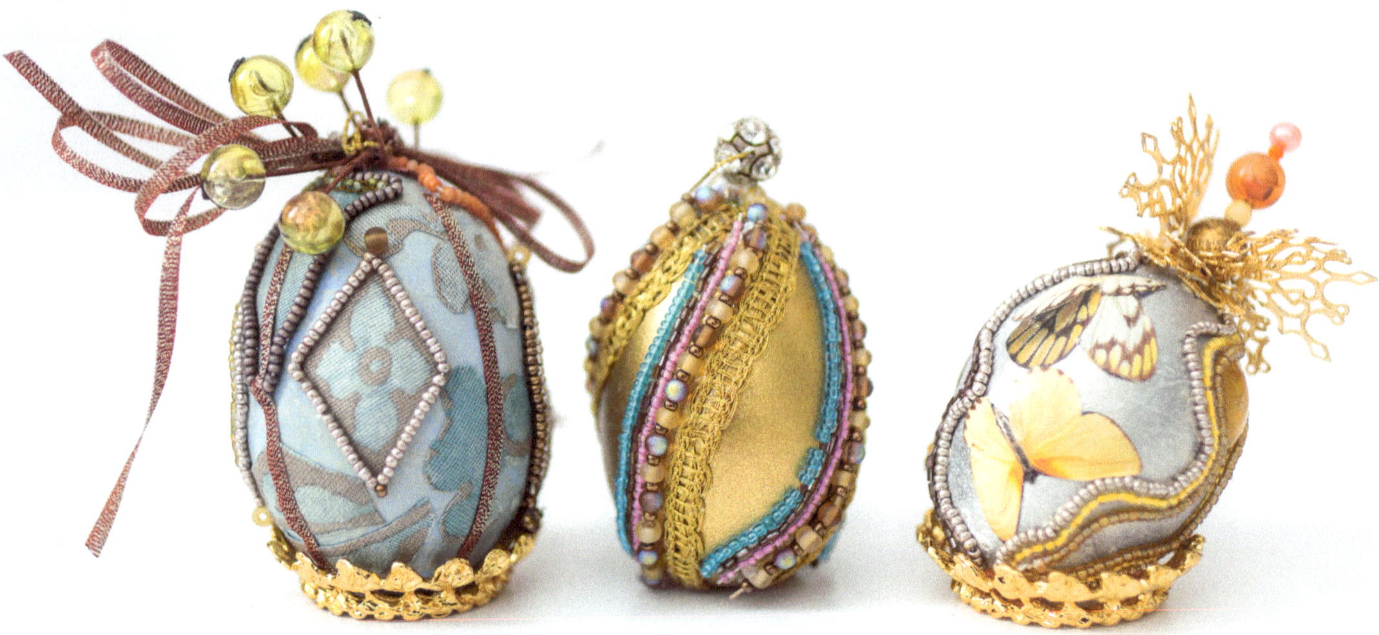

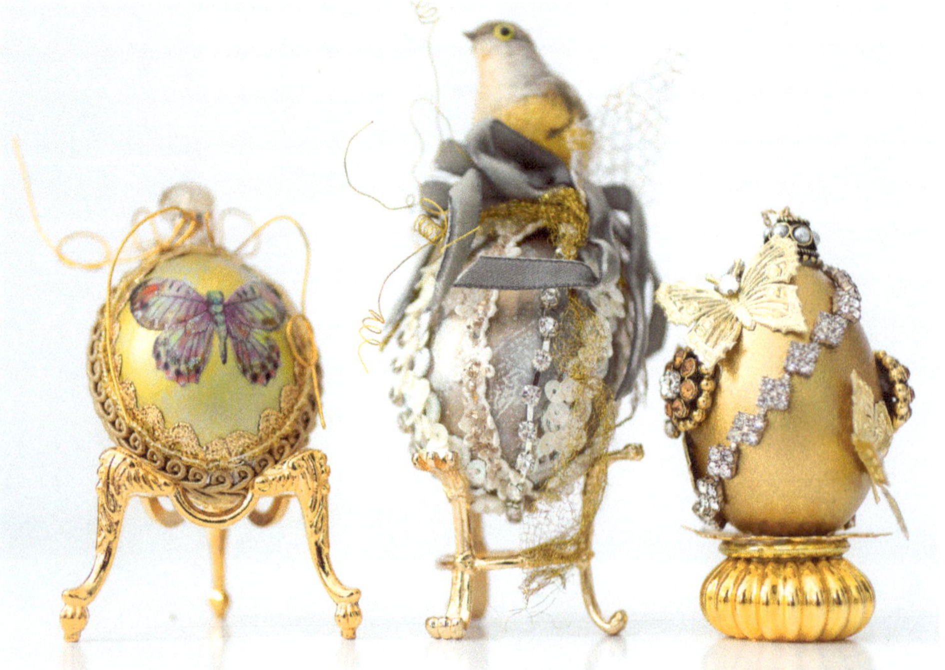

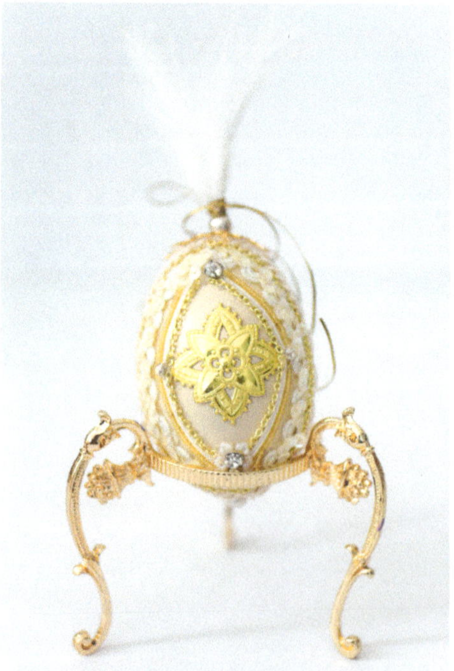

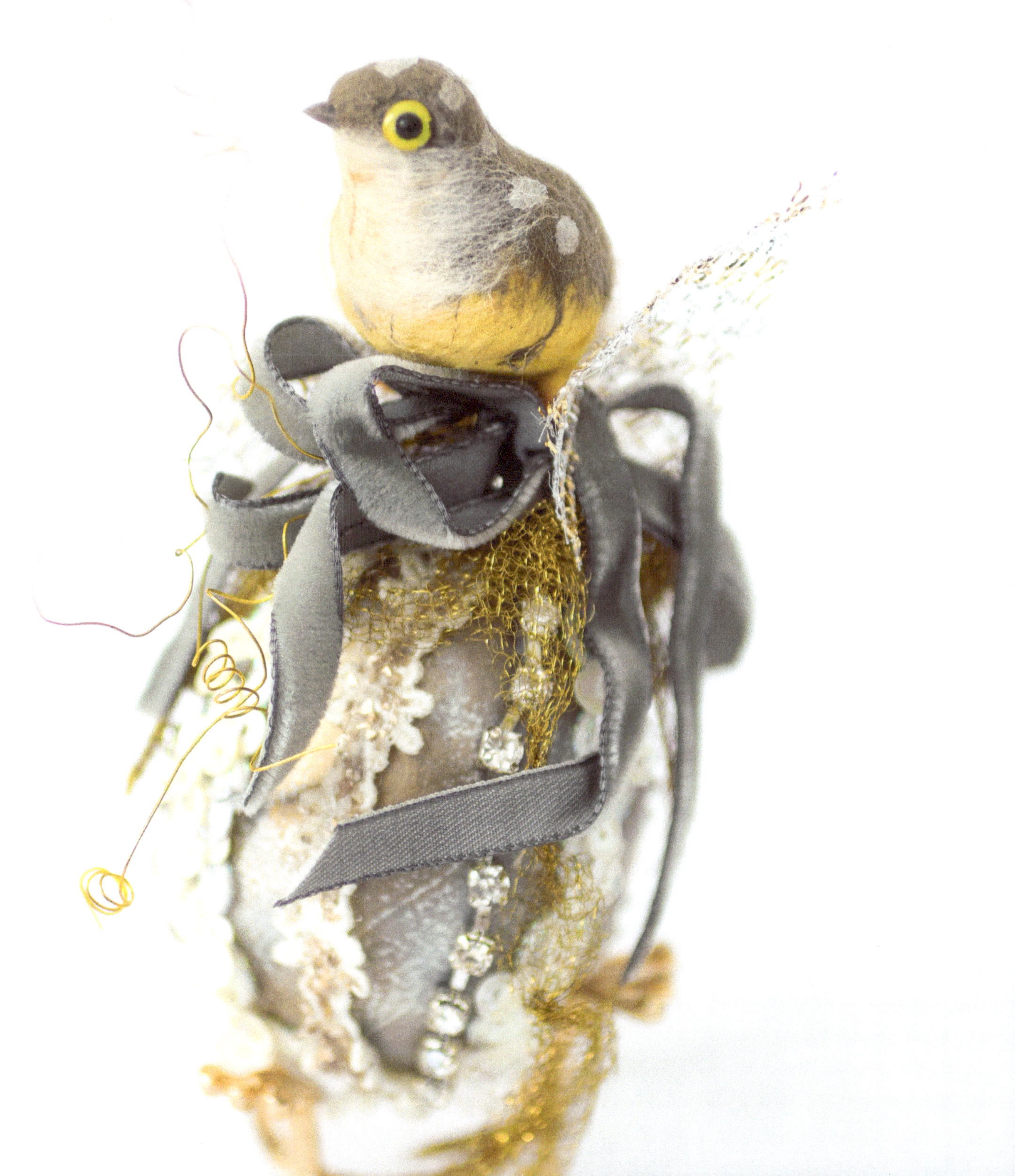

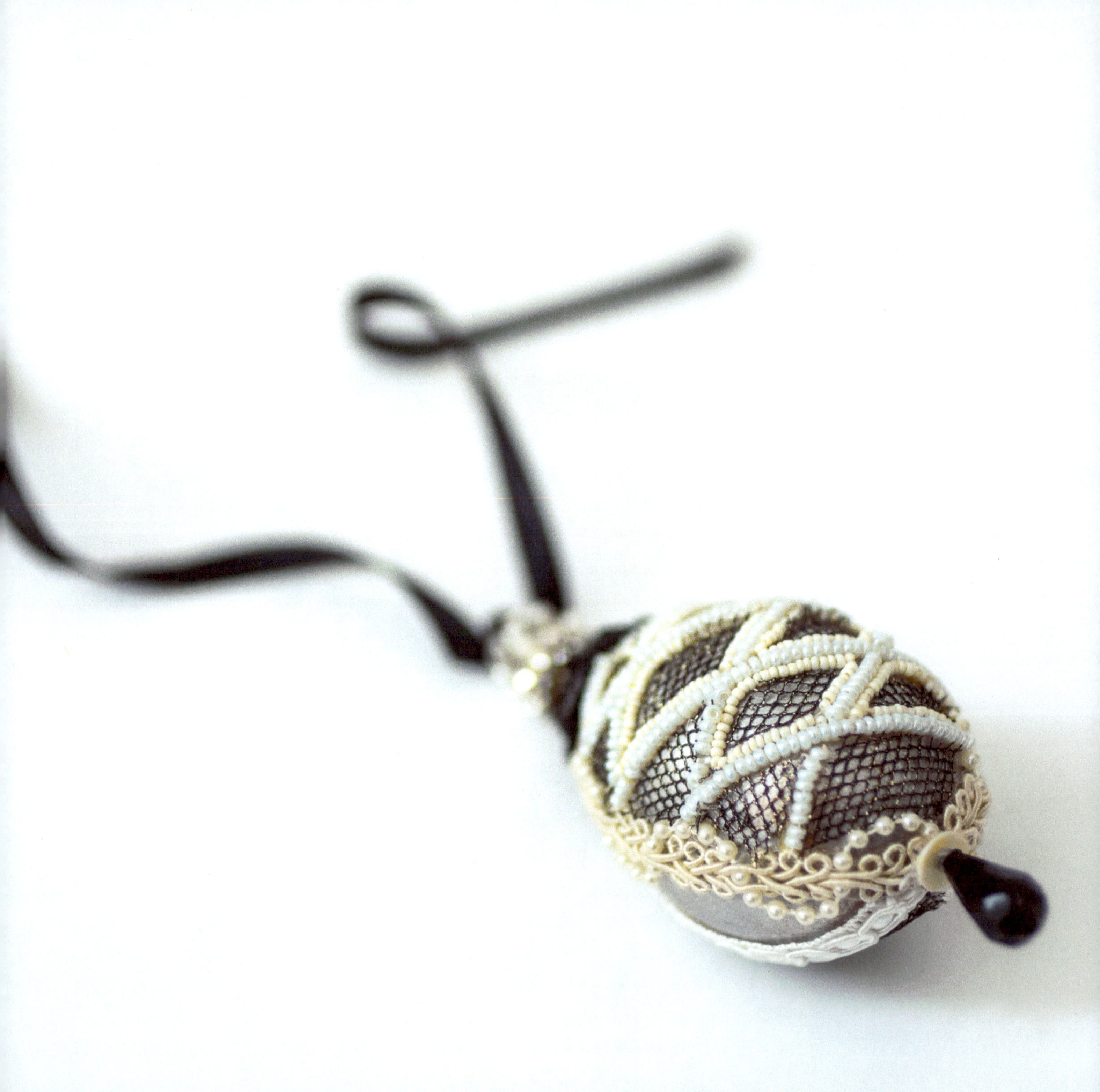

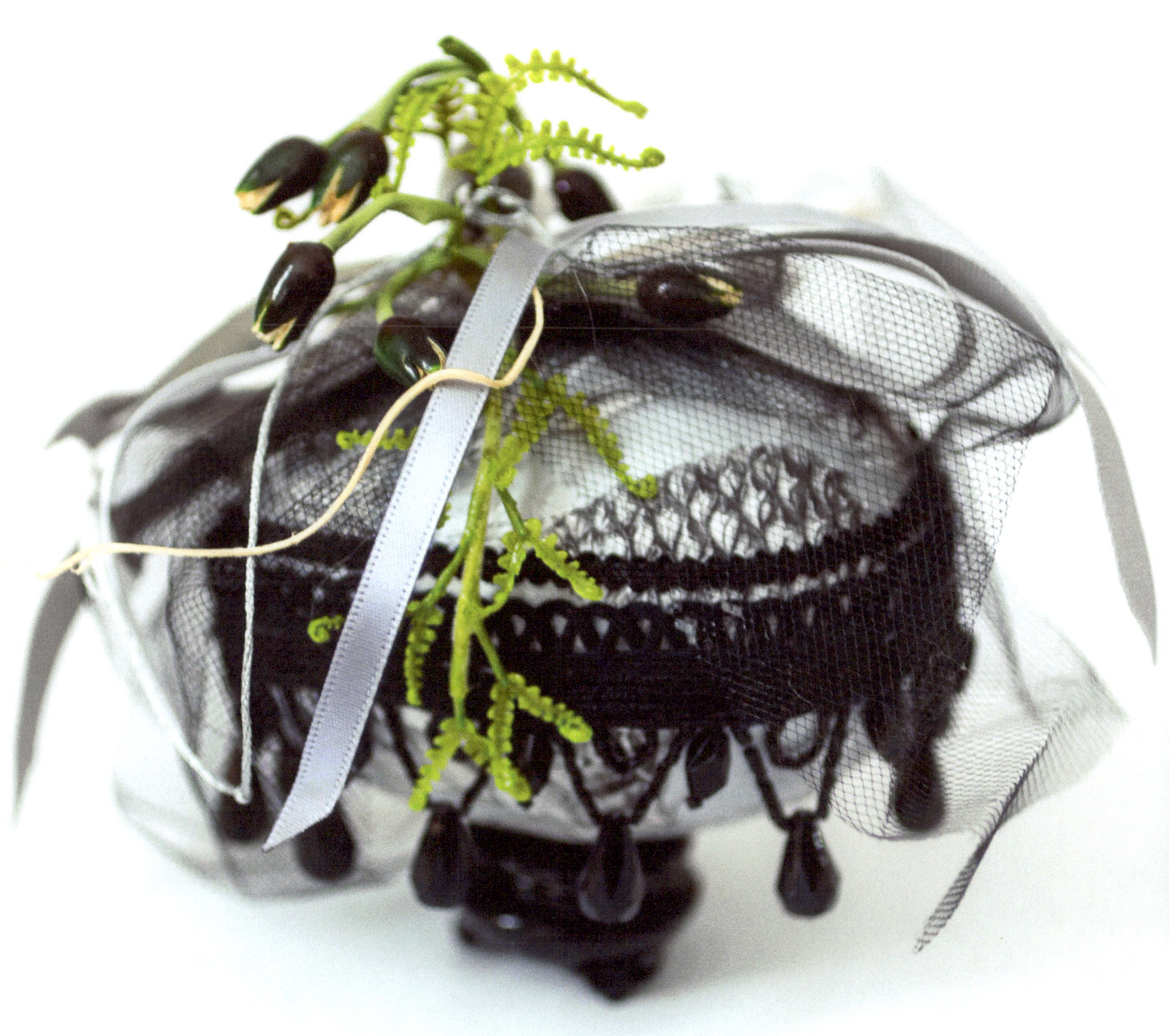

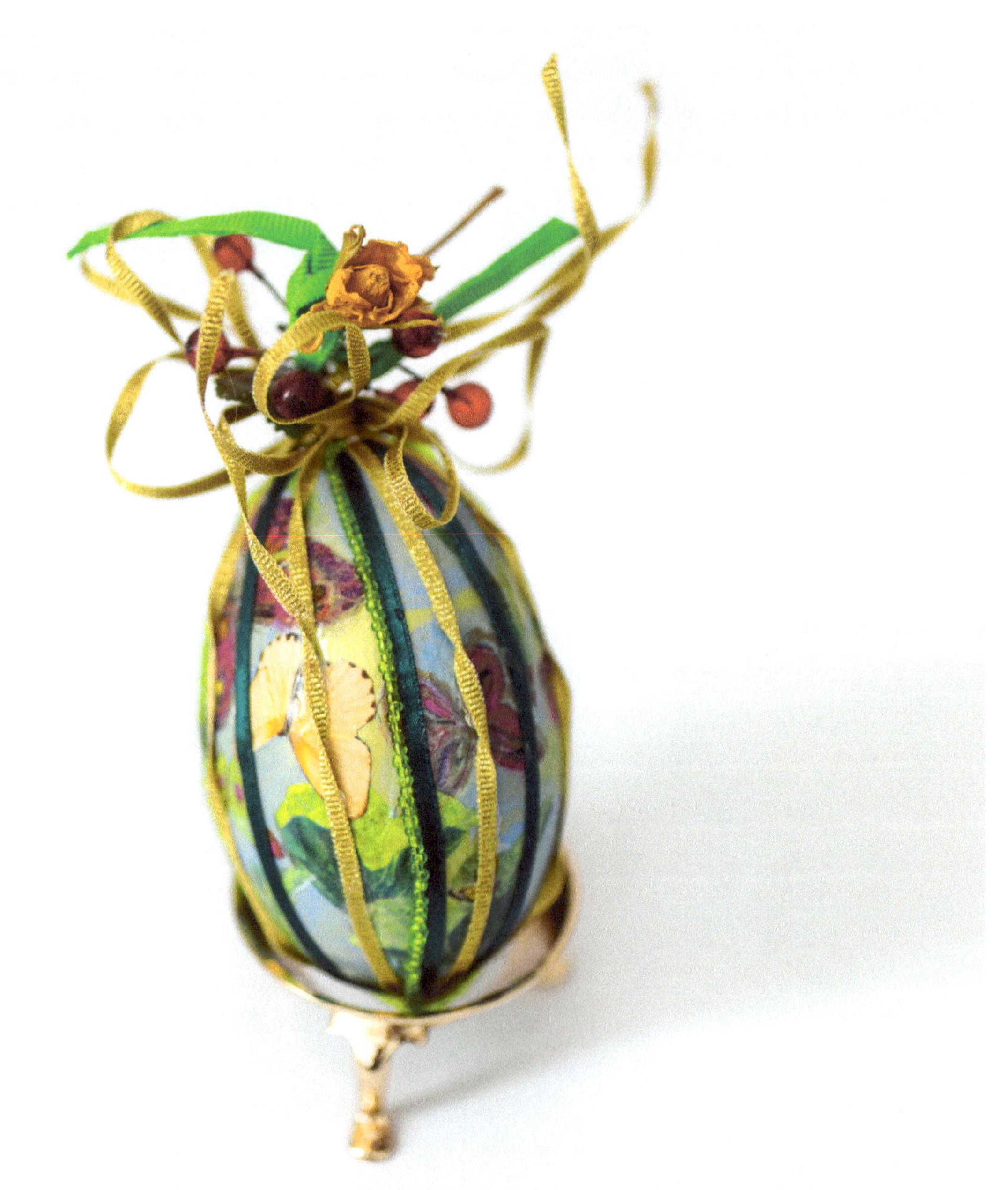

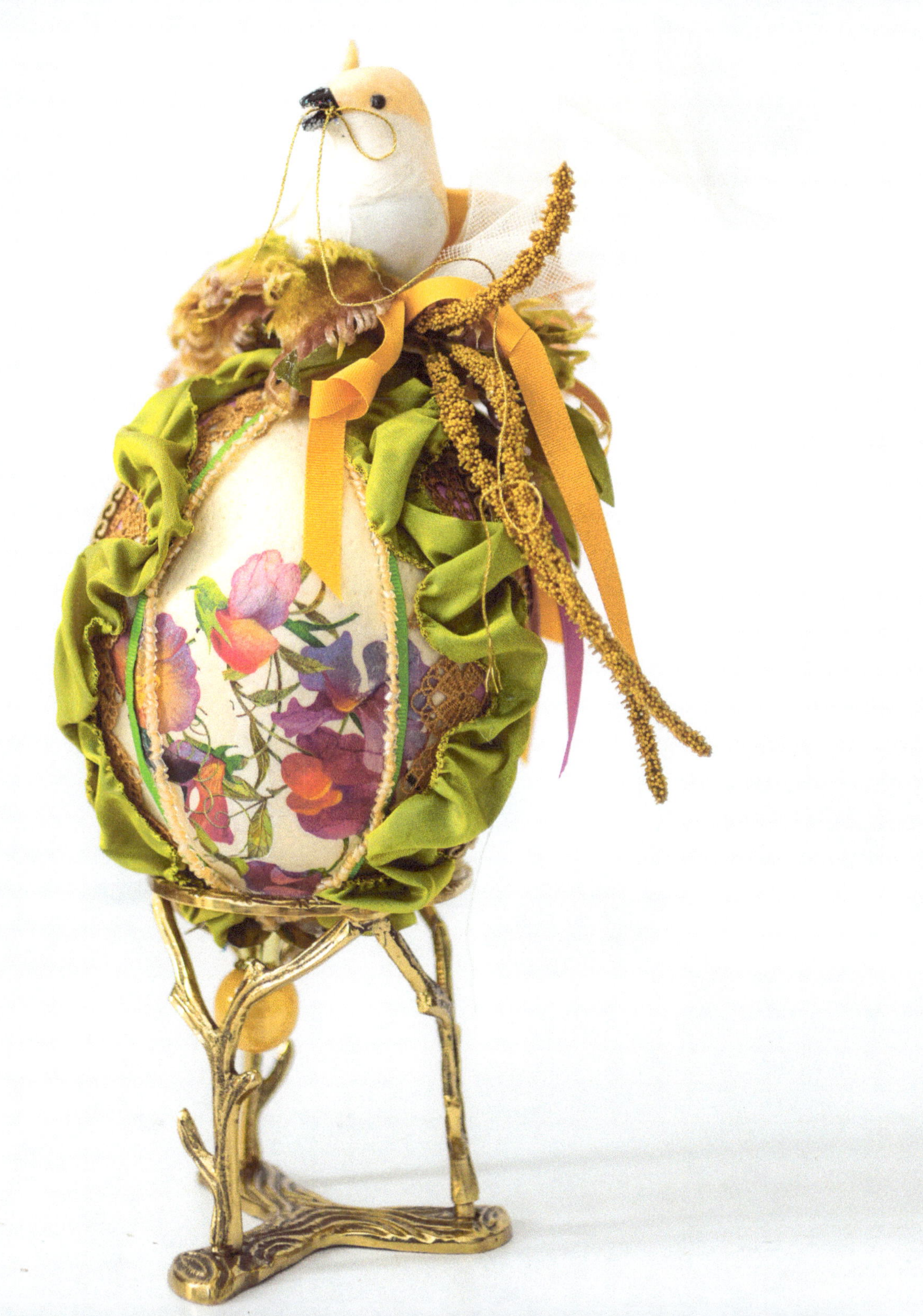

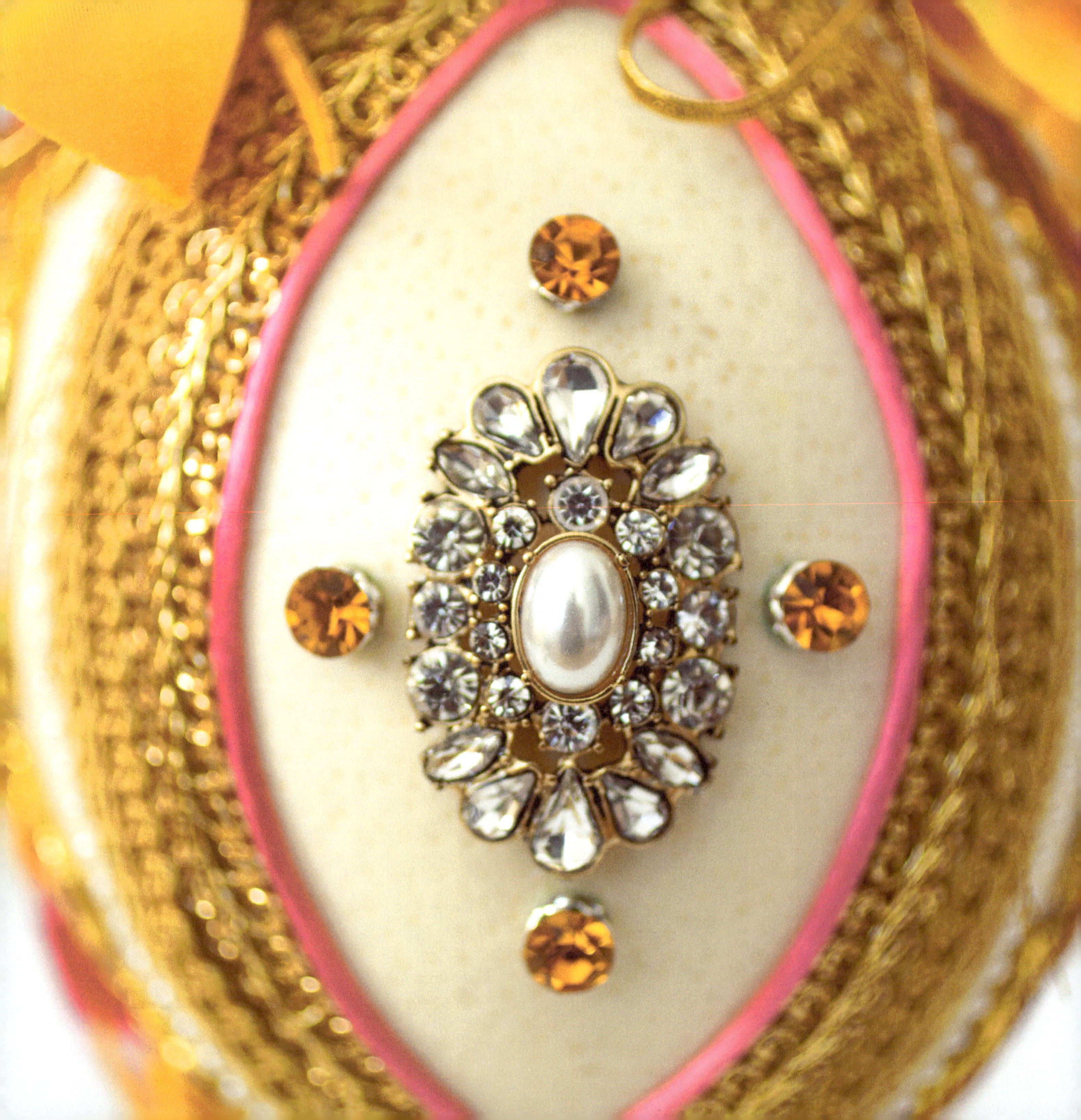

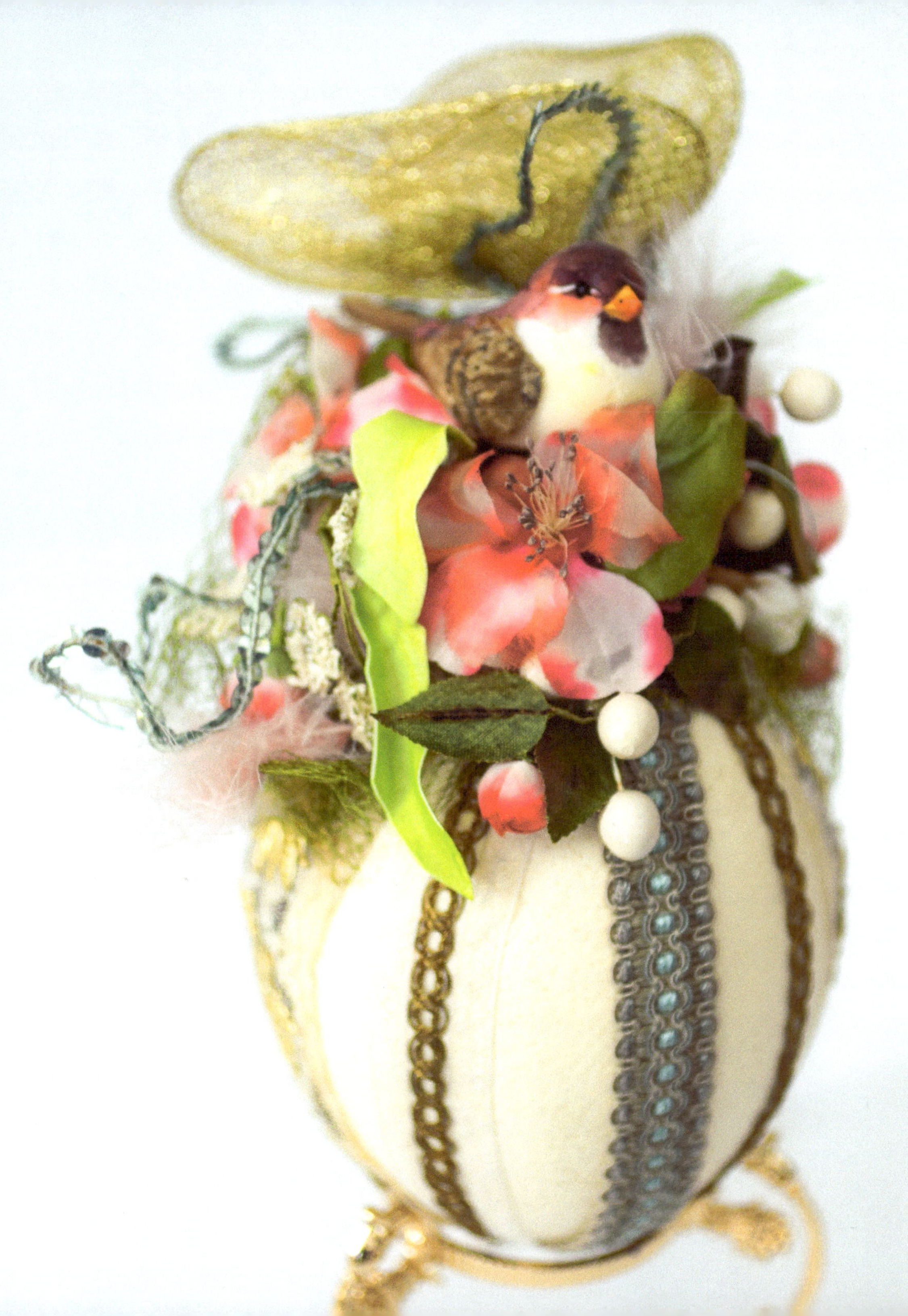

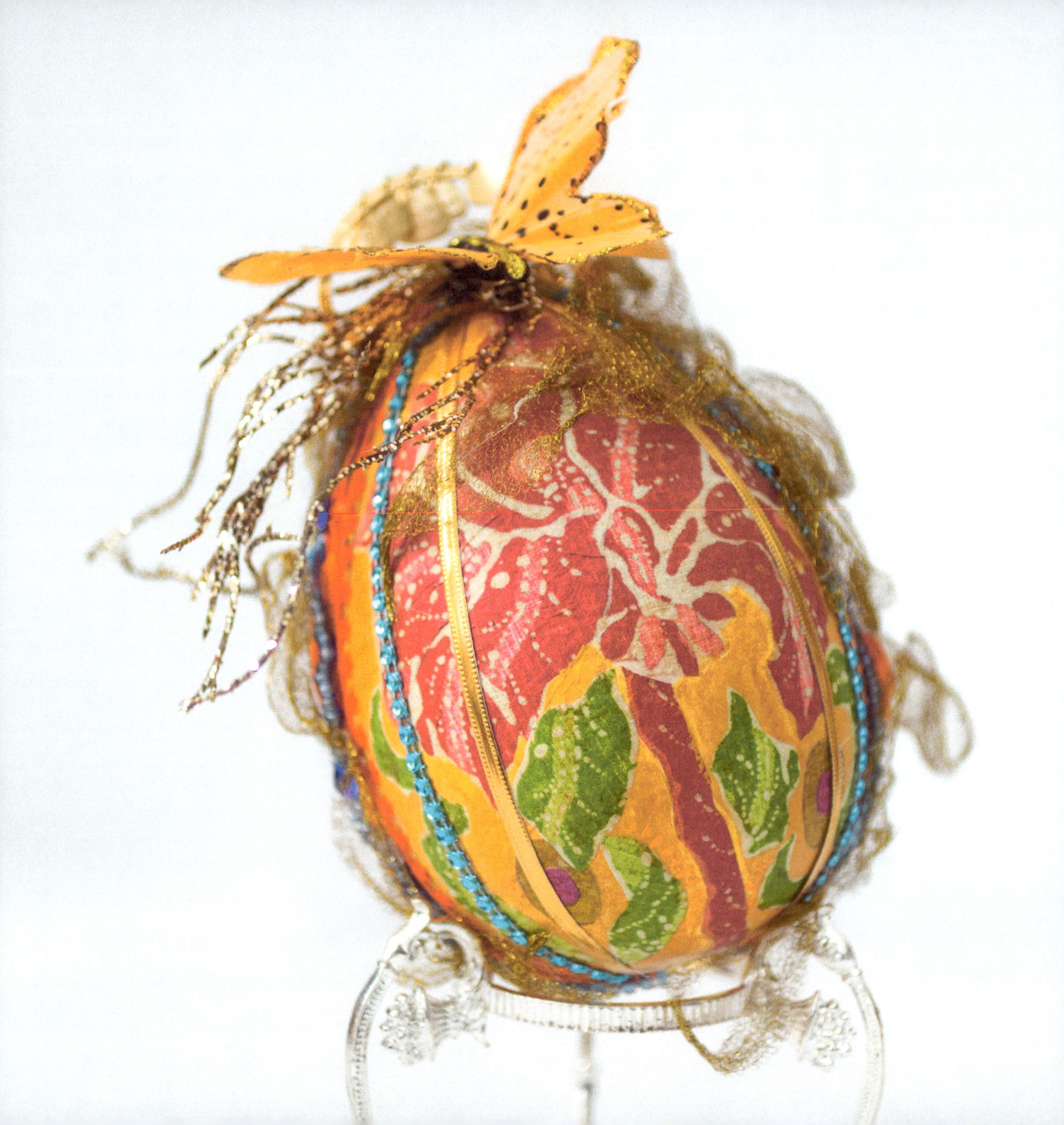

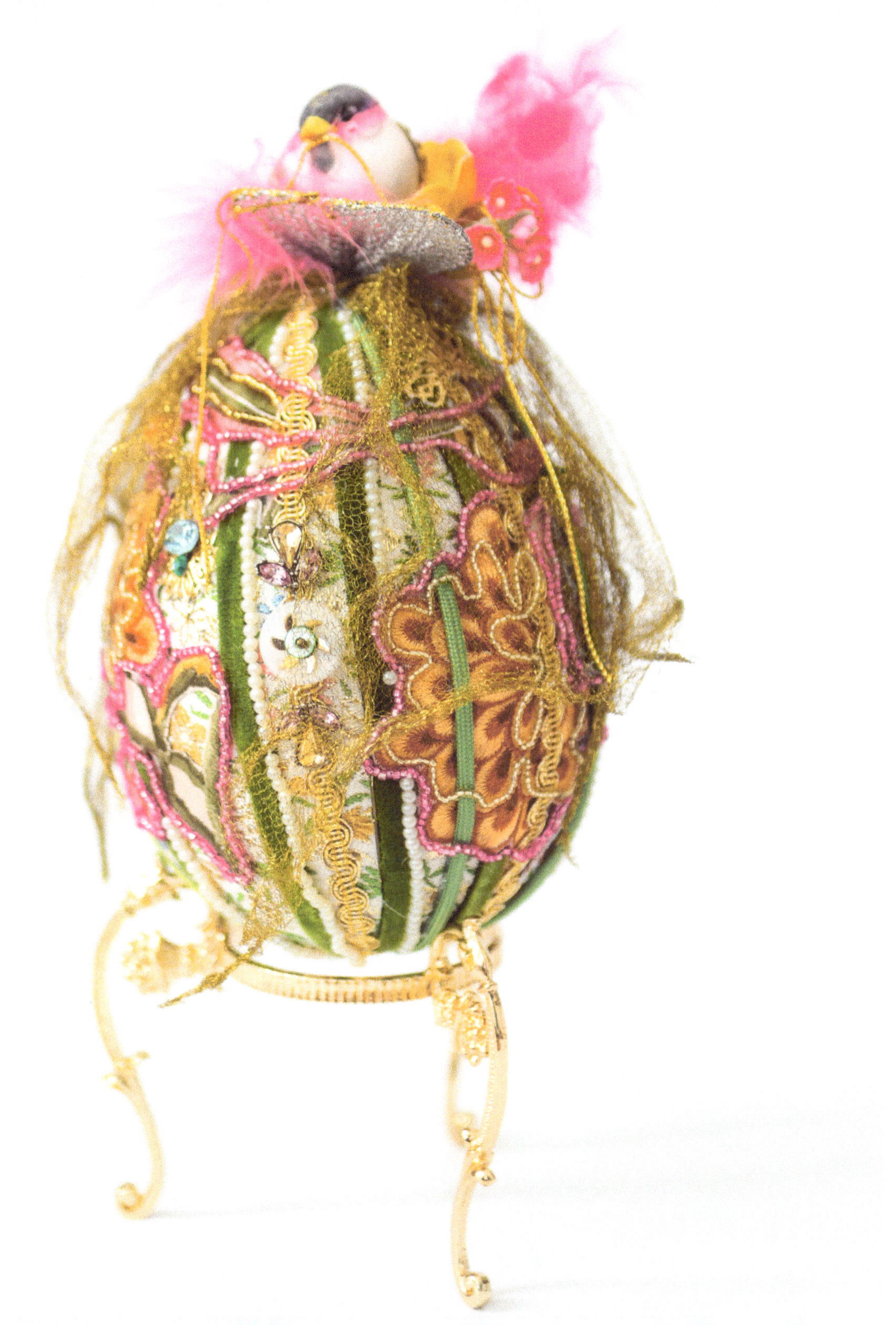

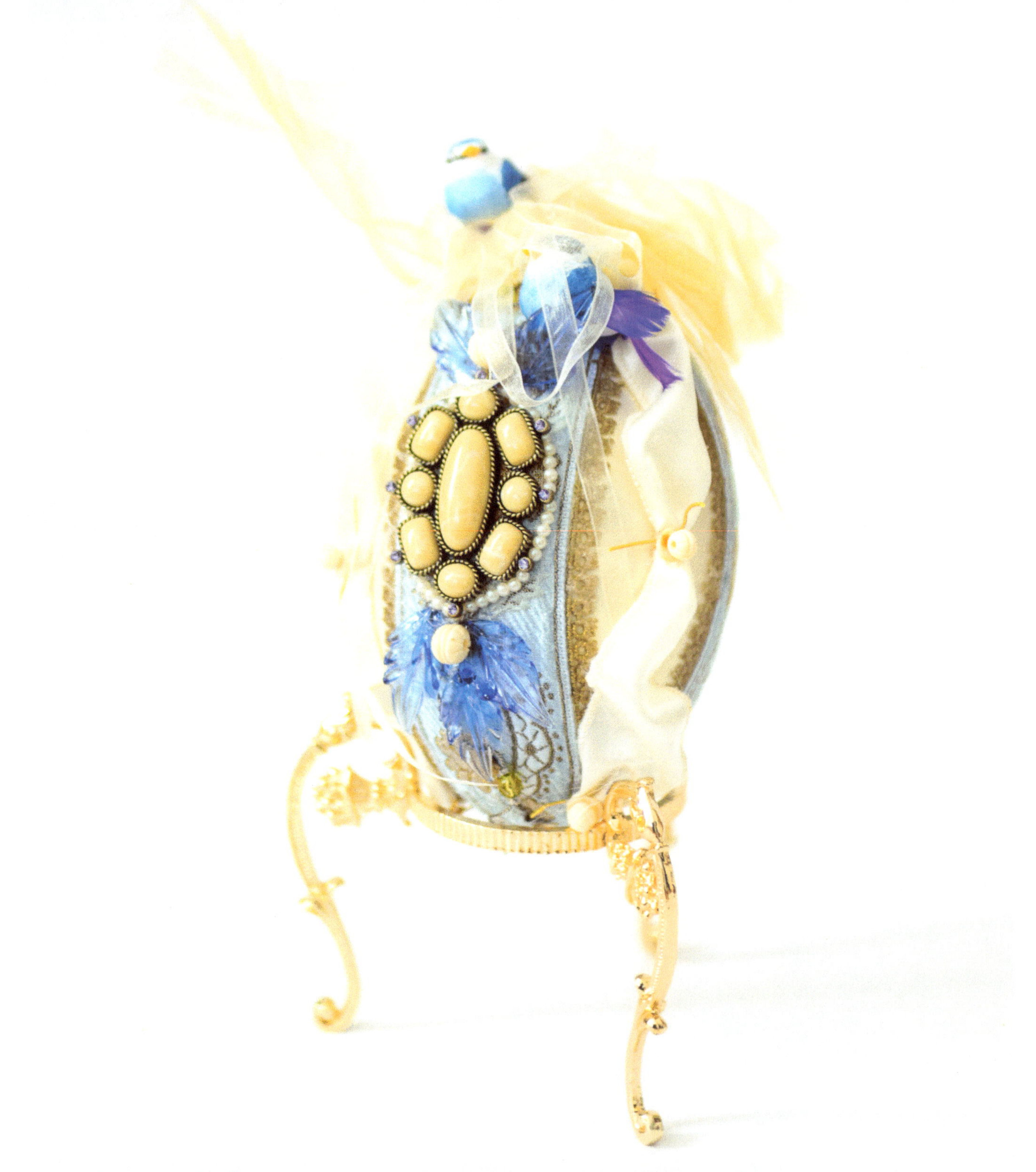

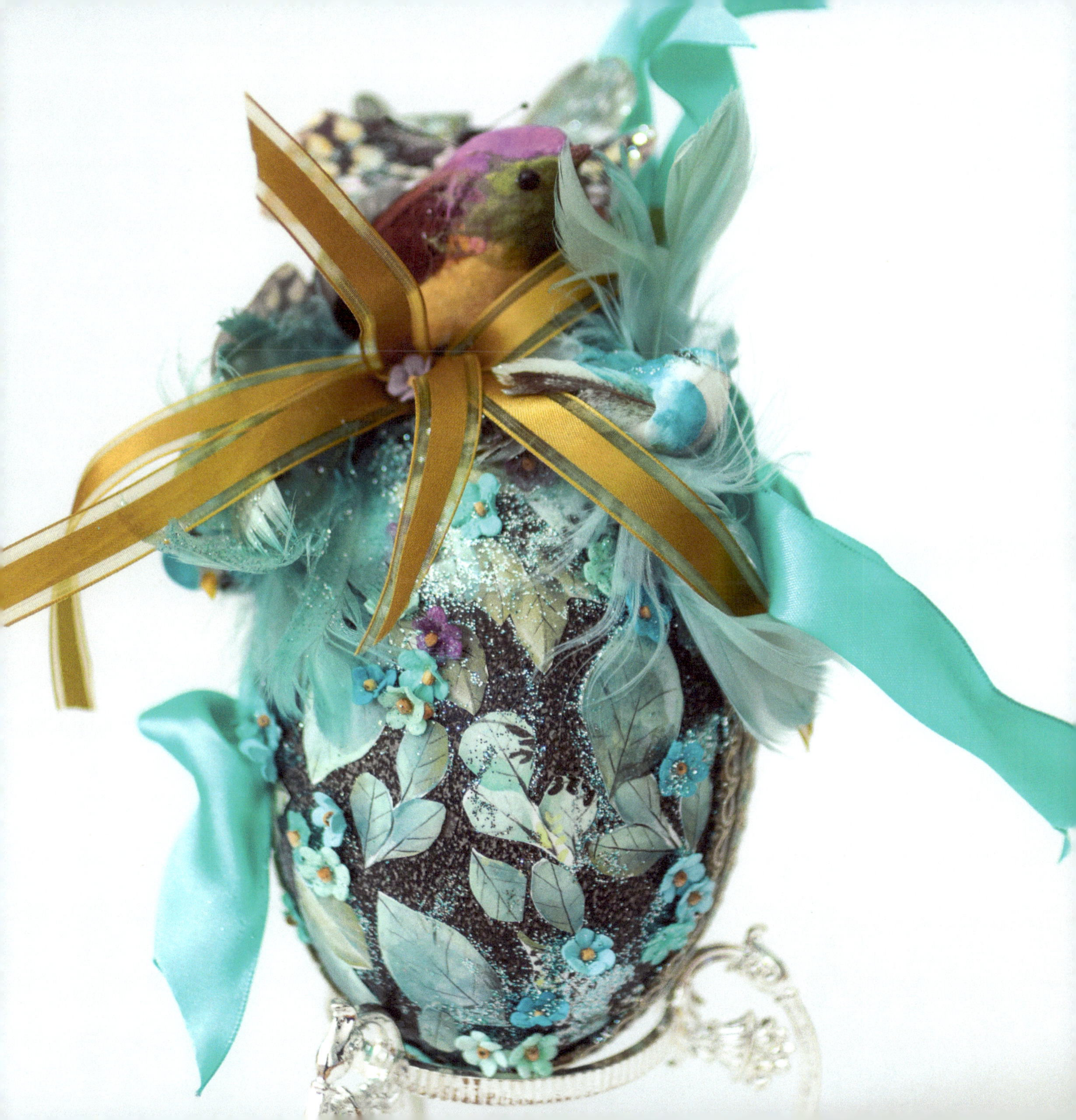

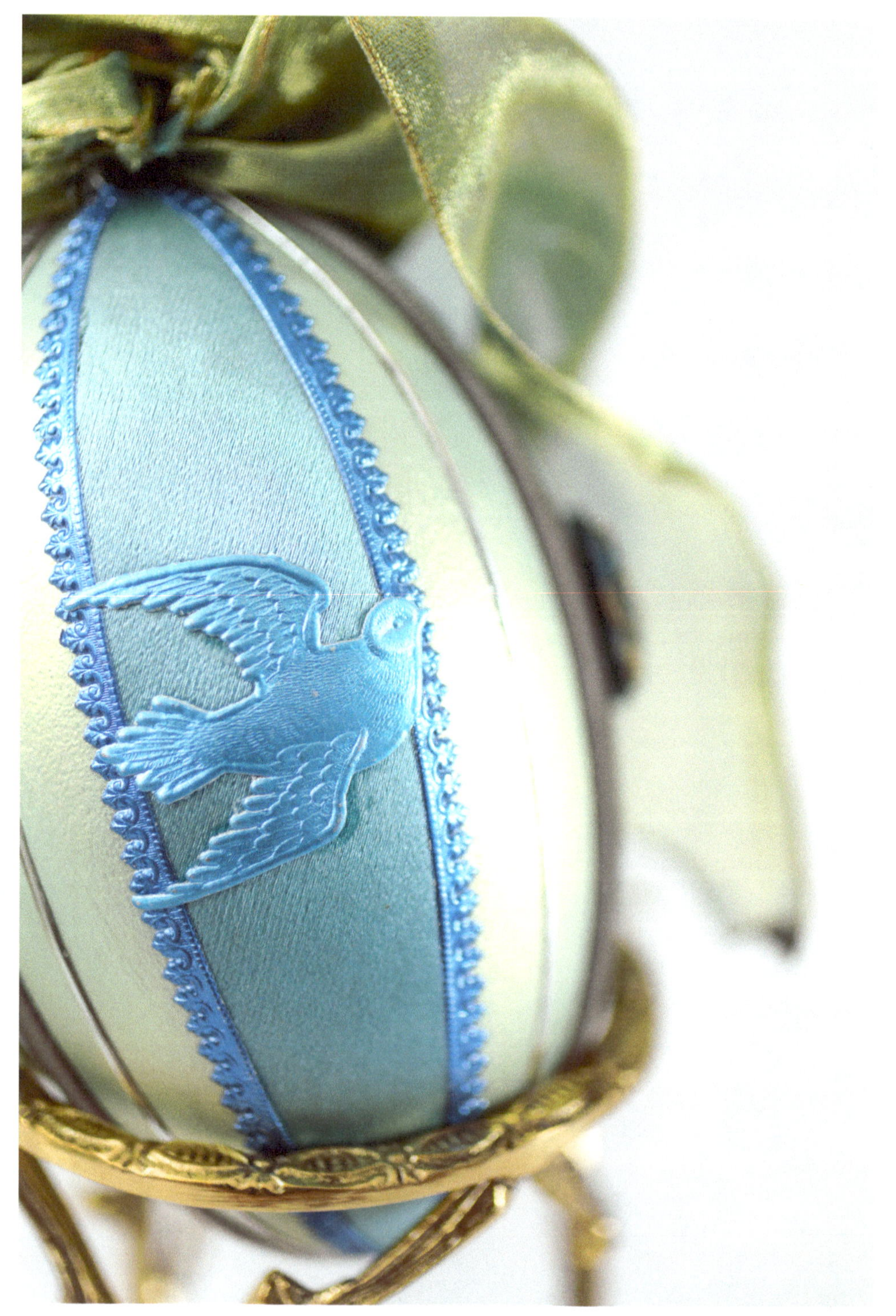

Works Cited

Birkhead, Tim. *The Most Perfect Thing: Inside (and Outside) a Bird's Egg*. Bloomsbury, 2017.

Brookland, Natalie. "Our Treasures: Bird Egg Collections in the Whangārei Museum Archives Valuable Research Tool." *NZ Herald*, NZ Herald, 1 Oct. 2020, https://www.nzherald.co.nz/northern-advocate/news/our-treasures-bird-egg-collections-in-whanga-rei-museum-archives-valuable-research-tool/6JYJOOEA2UVLRJXCDLDRWZUGMY/.

Brown, Margaret Wise. *The Golden Egg Book*. Illustrated by Leonard Weisgard, Little Golden Books - Random House Children's Books, 1947.

Golembiewski, Kate. "The Lost Victorian Art of Egg Collecting." *The Atlantic*, Atlantic Media Company, 25 Mar. 2016, https://www.theatlantic.com/science/archive/2016/03/the-lost-victorian-art-of-egg-collecting/475476/.

Hall, Stephanie. "The Ancient Art of Decorating Eggs." *The Ancient Art of Decorating Eggs | Folklife Today*, The Library of Congress, 6 Apr. 2017, https://blogs.loc.gov/folklife/2017/04/decorating-eggs/.

Ohrbach, Barbara Milo, et al. *The Scented Room: Cherchez's Book of Dried Flowers, Fragrance, and Potpourri.* Clarkson Potter, 1986.

Pavid, Katie. "A Journey through the Largest Egg Collection in the World." *Collections - Natural History Museum*, The Trustees of The Natural History Museum, London, https://www.nhm.ac.uk/discover/news/2018/march/a-journey-through-the-largest-egg-collection-in-the-world.html.

Rude, Emelyn. "The Forgotten History of 'Hen Fever'." *Culture*, National Geographic, 3 May 2021, https://www.nationalgeographic.com/culture/article/the-forgotten-history-of-hen-fever.

Smorodinova, G. G., et al. *Fabergé and the Russian Master Goldsmiths*. Edited by Gerald Hill, Hugh Lauter Levin Associates, 1989.

Walker, Rob. *The Art of Noticing: 131 Ways to Spark Creativity, Find Inspiration, and Discover Joy in the Everyday*. Knopf, 2019.

Sourcing

There are many sources, domestic and international, which specialize in supplies for egg artistry. One of the sources I have used recently is The Eggers Nest at Bracken Ridge Ranch, where all eggs are from domestically raised birds. Visit brackenridgeranch.com.

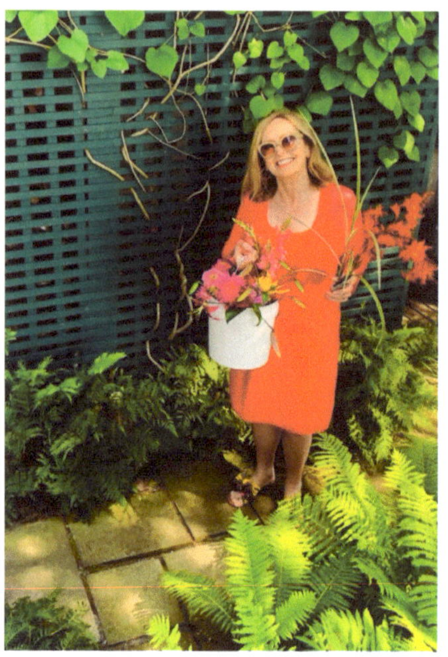

Isabel B. Anthony is the maker behind *The Exquisite Egg*, editor of *Garland County, Arkansas: Our History and Heritage*, and author of *Delicious Memories: Five Generations of Family Recipes*. A native Arkansan, Isabel remembers her first creative endeavor: sticking seashells on a picture frame at age five. Later, stitchery, sewing, and painting classes inspired her to pursue a bachelor of fine arts degree, focusing on graphic design and art history. Following a multi-faceted visual arts career in Dallas, she operated a women's clothing store in Hot Springs, Arkansas. Never without a small studio, the artist's embellishment of Easter eggs has brought her pleasure for over sixty years. Isabel lives and creates in Little Rock, close to her family, her studio, her books and a stray cat, Winslow.

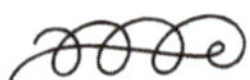

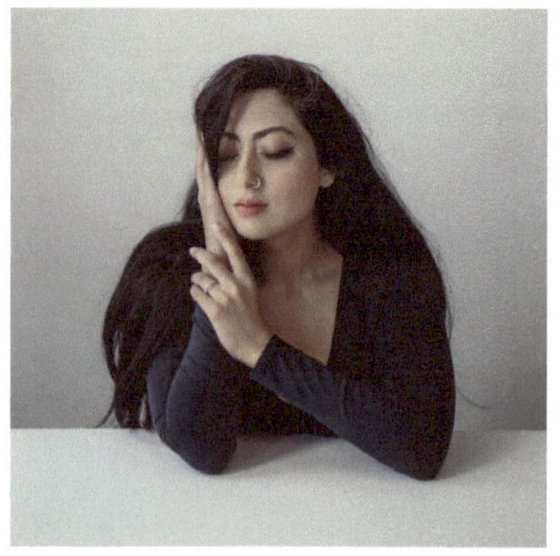

Arshia Khan, photographer of *The Exquisite Egg*, is a Little Rock-based editorial photographer and visual storyteller specializing in portraiture and food photography. Find her images in her book, *The Modern Arkansas Table*, as well as in the pages of *Southern Living Magazine*, *Bon Appétit*, *Food Network Magazine*, *Outside Magazine*, and National Geographic Books. Arshia is often found hiking, knitting, making ceramics, or eating ice cream. She is available for work worldwide. Find her at arshiakhan.net.